HOW TO GET THE BEST
ROM THE 1911 CENSUS

by John Hanson FSG

SOCIETY OF GENEALOGISTS ENTERPRISES LTD

Published by
Society of Genealogists Enterprises Limited
14 Charterhouse Buildings, Goswell Road
London EC1M 7BA

© The Society of Genealogists Enterprises 2009.

ISBN: 978-1-907199-00-4

British Library Cataloguing in Publication Data
A CIP Catalogue record for this book is available from the British Library.

The Society of Genealogists Enterprises Limited is a wholly owned
subsidiary of the Society of Genealogists, a registered charity, no 233701.

About the Author

John retired in 2001 having been a systems specialist in the banking industry for many years. His main interest is in the use of computers for family history and the uses that the internet can be put to as an aid in research.

He now lecturers on family history all over the country, writes for several of the genealogical magazines and also teaches the subject locally in Milton Keynes. As a member of the Society of Genealogists for many years he has served on most of the committees and as a Trustee. For "services to genealogy" he was made a Fellow of the Society of Genealogists in 2005. He is a member of the Guild of One-Name Studies and also data manager for The Halsted Trust.

Together with Jeanne Bunting he has been offering computer and research advice at fairs and events all round the country for many years. More recently they were joined by Graham Walter and the three of them became the Census Detectives. See www.censusdetectives.org.uk

Cover Image - Foreground: 1911 Census Record (Alfred Charles Donovan Apperly). © Crown copyright, image reproduced courtesy of The National Archives. Background: Photograph from the Baker-Holl special collection at Society of Genealogists (Oxford High Street c.1911).

Facsimiles of Crown copyright records in The National Archives of the UK appear by permission of the Controller of HM Stationery Office.

PREFACE

The aim of this book is to help you get the best from the website of the newly released 1911 census for England and Wales. It is also worth remembering that the 1911 is radically different from all the census returns that we have seen in the past.

The information contained within this book is based on the site as at the time of publication and every effort has been made to ensure that it is as up to date as possible. However the site is still evolving and new material and features are still being added, which may affect the details published here. It is possible that the site may change but it is hoped that by leaving the writing until now, the site has settled down with the exception of the material still to be added.

Each part of the site will be explained in detail together with hints and tips about trying to get the best from the site.

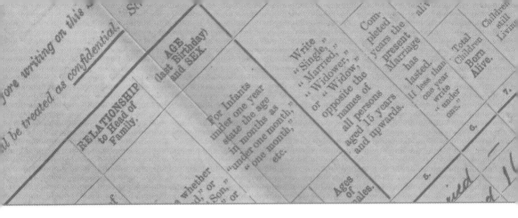

ACKNOWLEDGEMENTS

I am indebted to the help and advice from my fellow "Census Detective" Jeanne Bunting and also to Sue Gibbons who took the book to task and corrected my English.

Without the help, advice and support provided by FindMyPast in the production of this book it would not have been possible.

CONTENTS

FIGURES

CHAPTER 1
About the 1911 census online

In recent times the census returns have been released on the first working day in January after it has been closed for 100 years. Therefore the last one released under this system was the 1901 census on 2 January 2002. There had been much speculation over the past few years as to whether the original intention in 1901 had been to keep it closed for 100 years.

The early release

Back in 2006 a complaint was lodged with the Information Commissioner's Office (www.ico.gov.uk), under the Freedom of Information Act, contesting The National Archives intention not to release the 1911 census before 2012. Searching the ICO website for "1911 census" will reveal the full story but in essence the ruling on 11 December states - "The Commissioner requires the National Archives to disclose the requested information to the complainant.". It went on to say "The Commissioner stresses that that this Decision must be confined to the circumstances relating to the information requested in this case. This is not - and cannot be - a decision that the entirety of the 1911 census must now be disclosed. Nor does it create any precedent in the sense that all other requests for specific information within the 1911 or other census schedules

must succeed. This Decision concludes with more general guidance about situations where section 41 of the Act may apply in this context. Each request for 1911 census information will need to be treated separately on its merits."

The search service that was set up by The National Archives to make the census available under the FOI access ruling cost £45 per address and was based solely on the address of the property and was not searchable by name. So if you could be sure that the address was right and you really needed to see the return early you could get it.

The minutes of the meeting of the Lord Chancellor's Advisory Council on National Records and Archives on the 1 February 2007 states "The council received a report on the response of The National Archives to the decision of the Information Commissioner that most of the information in the 1911 Census should be available earlier than the planned release date in 2012. A paid search service had been established which was satisfying the demand for information, and the project to digitise the records had been brought forward so that the bulk of the census could be released on-line, starting in 2009." (www.nationalarchives.gov.uk/ advisorycouncil/meetings/1feb07.htm)

For some years now major datasets, like the census, have been released in partnership with a commercial organisation. On the 11 April 2007 The National Archives announced that "The National Archives is delighted to announce that ScotlandOnline will partner the UK government's official archive in the forthcoming project to put the 1911 census for England and Wales online." (www.nationalarchives.gov.uk/news/stories/156.htm)

The early release of the 1911 census will, of course, have caused some problems. The originally contracted schedule for making it available that ScotlandOnline had negotiated on had been suddenly been reduced by 3 years.

In December 2007 findmypast.com was acquired by ScotlandOnline. The full details of the merger can be found at www.findmypast.com/media/ news/findmypast-scotland-online-family-history.jsp. In July 2008 the new combined company was renamed as brightsolid and again details of this can be found at www.findmypast.com/media/news/brightsolid-rebranding.jsp

This late merger has meant that the look and feel of the web site is much more in the manner of ScotlandsPeople rather than the usual Findmypast.com style. The infrastructure of the whole process and design being past the point of no return.

Where is it available?

The 1911 census is currently only available on a dedicated web site www.1911census.co.uk. The site was first released to a limited number of people (in fact about 72,000) for beta (pre-launch) testing on 18 December, 2008. During the testing period, which continued for about two weeks, feedback was encouraged to ensure that the site was as prepared for the final public launch as it could be.

The site had its public launch on Tuesday 13 January, 2009 and everyone held their breath not wanting a repeat of what happened with the 1901 census back in 2002. However, all the prior testing of the site had meant that sufficient plans could be made to ensure that the servers to access the site would not "fall over".

The site was also heavily restricted as to what you could search for in those early days, the new features being released slowly to reduce their impact on the system. At its release it was estimated that about 80% of the final data was there and included all of the counties in England from Lancashire and the West Riding of Yorkshire southwards.

The contract between ScotlandOnline and The National Archives means that the 1911 census will be exclusively available only through them until at least 6 months after the last piece number is made available online. After that anyone can apply to The National Archive to purchase a set of the images. Anyone buying the images with the intention of providing an online service will also need to transcribe them from scratch.

Is there any new information in this census?

The Government of the early twentieth century was becoming increasingly concerned about the falling birth rate and additional questions were asked about infant mortality and fertility in marriage. The questions were very carefully worded and only supposed to be completed by married women. Husbands, widows, unmarried or divorced women were not supposed to complete the information, but many did. The inclusion of these questions relating to the length of the existing marriage, number of children born and died obviously caused much confusion and is explained in more detail in Chapter 6.

Moreover, some additional information was collected in relation to a person's occupation, with information being collected for the first time, for everyone over the age of ten, about the 'Industry or Service' that they were employed in. So you will be able to tell the type of warehouse in which your ancestor was a night watchman.

A change was also made in relation to the place of birth, particularly if it was outside England and Wales, and people were asked to state whether they were a Visitor or a Resident in this country.

What is different about this census?

Unless you are new to family history we are all aware of the format of the existing census material for England and Wales that is already online. This consists of the Enumerators Books that were made up from the schedules completed by the householders. The original schedules were destroyed at the time so all that we are left with is the transcription by the enumerator.

With the 1911 census the Enumerator left a schedule with each head of household. There are a total of 22 different schedule types and details as well as examples of them all can be found on the University of Essex 'Online Historical Population Reports' web site www.histpop.org. Not the easiest of web sites to find things on, but a mine of useful information, so you might want to try http://preview.tinyurl.com/d4f24j which will direct you to the correct page.

The Enumerator returned on Monday 3 April to collect the form. He had to check that the schedule had been completed correctly and gather any missing information. This is basically the way that it happened in the previous censuses.

From this is point on is where it changes though. The schedules (which form class RG14 at The National Archives) were left as they were and some of the information was entered into the Enumerators Summary Books (which form class RG78 at The National Archives). Once completed both were forwarded to the statistics office for the information to be extracted. This again was a new departure, using machinery for the first time to collate the information. It is because machinery was used that the places of birth and occupation have had numerical values attached to them on the census schedules.

There have been a number of interesting articles in the genealogical press since its release and I would draw particular attention to those in Ancestors Magazine issue 79 which had a number of articles relating to the 1911 census and in particular the process that it went through to be made available over the Internet.

Statistics about the 1911 census

The 1911 census is a huge set of records - more than 12 times the size of the 1901 census - with over 8 million schedules covering our 36 million ancestors. It comprises 35,000 volumes and occupies some 2 kilometres of shelving at the

National Archives at Kew. They are generally in good condition and suitable for scanning, with less than 5 per cent requiring more extensive conservation work before they could be scanned safely. In addition there are also 38,000 volumes of Enumerators' Summary Books that are in excellent condition and provide valuable supporting information.

The population recorded by the 1911 census was 36,075,269, an increase of 3,547,426 or 11% over the 1901 census. The county with the largest increase in population was Middlesex with a staggering 42%. On the other hand the City and the Metropolitan Boroughs of the County of London (as it then was) recorded a small drop.

Has it all been included?

Everything has been included from the original schedules and Enumerator Summary Books with the exception of one column which has been 'redacted'. What they mean is that it has been withheld until the normal released date in 2012. The column relates to '… whether the person was deaf, dumb, lunatic, imbecile, etc' and is covered in Chapter 6 where we explore, in detail, the images and transcriptions.

Is there a cost involved?

Yes there is. The 1911 web site is a PayPerView one and no subscription option will be available on this site. Sometime later in 2009 it will become available on the main findmypast.com website as part of a subscription package. At present no details of the possible cost are available.

To use the 1911 census web site you need to purchase credits. The cost is 10 credits per household transcript and 30 credits to look at the corresponding image. The cost of purchasing credits varies depending on the package that you purchase and details are in Chapter 5. You do need to register to look at images and transcriptions and again this is covered in Chapter 5 but basic searches of the indexes are completely free of charge.

Whilst these costs (between £2.40 and £3.50 per image) may seem to be high you have to bear in mind that for the price of the image you will actually receive up to 8 images of the Householder's schedule and the Enumerators Summary Books, all in full colour. The advantage of this is that it makes them much easier to read. Add to that the fact that there doesn't seem to be the level of crossings out by the statisticians which made entries so difficult to read in previous censuses!

What about Scotland and Ireland?

The census material released in 2009 covers England & Wales. The censuses for Scotland and Ireland have always been separate and are the subject of legislation in their own countries.

Scotland will, one assumes, ultimately appear on the ScotlandsPeople website www.scotlandspeople.gov.uk (also maintained by brightsolid). They are covered by their own Freedom of Information rulings and it has already been stated that the 1911 census for Scotland will not be released early and we will have to wait until January 2012 for its release.

On the other hand, the Irish 1911, along with the 1901 census, has been available in microfilm format since the 1970's (they are the only complete surviving censuses for Ireland.) It is only recently that the 1911 Irish Census has begun to be indexed. It can be found at www.census.nationalarchives.ie

What about the later censuses?

The 1921 census and all later censuses remain in the custody of the Office for National Statistics and not The National Archives.

The 1921 census covered by the 1920 Census Act and will remain closed until 2022. The 1931 census was destroyed by fire during the Second World War and of course there was no census in 1941. Whether I shall live long enough to see myself on the 1951 census is a different story, but I hope so.

Where can I find out more about the census?

There is a new website which also has some interesting information on the 1911 census at www.1911census.org.uk.

CHAPTER 2
The Home Page

T he "home page", the normal starting point of any site, is there to provide the navigation round the whole site and should be the one bookmarked in your favourites list to come back to.

This is the home page of the 1911 census. We will examine the page in detail in this chapter and the following chapters will look at the use of each of the parts of the site that are of specific interest and need fuller explanations.

Figure 2-1 The home page before signing in

The line of tabs across the top of all pages allow you to navigate to the essential parts of the site.

home will always return you this "Home Page"

search the 1911 census takes you directly to the main search screen - this is covered in the next two chapters (3 and 4) which deal with the two specific types of search.

my records enables you to see the details of transcriptions and images that you have already viewed. There are a number of things that you can do with these as well as looking again at previously viewed pages without having to pay and these are covered in Chapter 7.

about the 1911 census has items about the history of the 1911 census as well as the current availability. You will also find useful information here about the codes, which we will examine later, relating to occupations and places of birth. Examples of each of the documents available are also included. There is also a brief section on "the world in 1911".

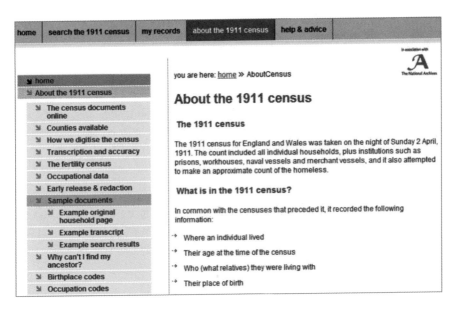

Figure 2-2 About the 1911 census

help & advice provides assistance with the general use of the site, much of which is covered in greater detail within this book.

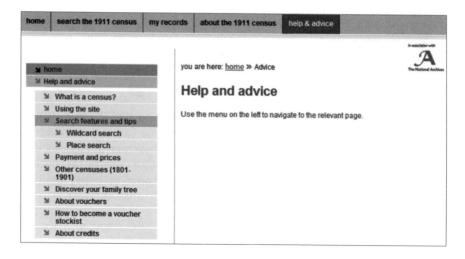

Figure 2-3 Help and advice

At the top of the screen

The 'sign in' link will sign you in automatically, if you have set it that way. If you aren't registered, which you need to be to look beyond the indexes, then the 'register link' will take you to the relevant screen. The 'buy credits' link only works if you are registered and signed in and takes you to the screen to buy more credits. All of these are covered again in chapter 5.

In the left hand panel

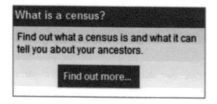

This has detailed explanations of what a census is, why it was taken and what they can tell you about your ancestors.

Discover your family tree

Are you new to family history? The 1911 census could be the first step of an exciting journey into your family's past.

Find out more...

This link is aimed at those people who haven't started tracing their family history yet. However I often find these refreshing to read, just to make sure that I haven't forgotten anything, especially with material that is new.

Payment Options

 Buy credits online using a credit or debit card for instant access to typed transcripts and images of original census documents

£ Order vouchers from our stockists
Activate vouchers

This link provides the ability to top up your credits. You can either buy credits online, order vouchers from a stockist, find a stockist or activate a voucher. These are covered in more detail in Chapter 5.

How it works

SEARCH FOR FREE

Search through the census index to find an ancestor, or to find out who lived in your house. This service is free.

PAY TO VIEW

Once you are sure of the record you want, you'll need to register and buy credits (see left) to view and print and save a typed transcript or an image of the original handwritten page.

In the centre, these links are just another way of getting to the main screens quickly.

The quick search

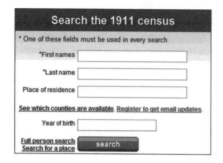

Figure 2-4   Quick search screen

Here you can do a 'quick search' and get an indication of the number of entries for the name you have entered. For a more detailed search click on 'Full person search' (covered in Chapter 3) or 'Search for a place' (covered in Chapter 4). You may be lucky and find exactly what you want with this initial search but it is highly unlikely, certainly not with the common names like John Smith (there are 22,931) or Mary Brown (9,836). In these cases you will be taken to the full search screen to refine the search as there are too many to display. If there are only a few then the search results will be displayed (this is covered in detail in Chapter 3).

You can't use wildcards in this search screen. If you try to you will be told that there are no records and be taken to the full search screen to amend your search. If you enter a 'year of birth' then the result will be based on a search of the year plus or minus one year.

At the bottom of the screen:

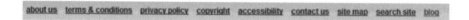

The only link that really needs explanation, and is certainly one that you need to check regularly, is the blog, which is found on the right hand end. A blog is "A personal or corporate website in the form of an online journal, with new entries appearing in sequence as they are written, especially as dealing with reflections or opinion, and typically incorporating links to other articles" (http://en.wiktionary.org/wiki/blog). It is the best way of keeping up to date with what is changing on the website and is where FindMyPast make announcements of the new material and features released in relation to the 1911 census.

When you are signed in the home page changes slightly. Details of how to sign in are covered in Chapter 5.

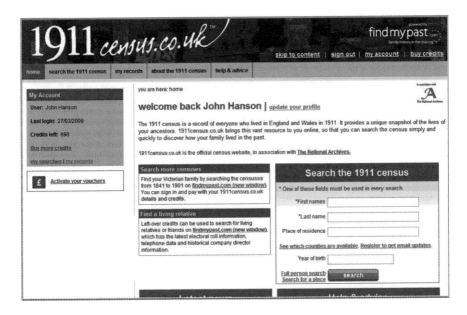

Figure 2-5 The home page after signing in

The top line now has a link to your account, details of which are covered in Chapter 5. In the centre the 'how it works' box has been replaced by two links which will take you to either the 'previous census' or 'living relatives' sections of the FindMyPast.com website.

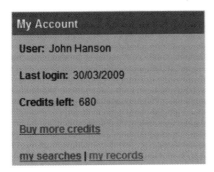

The left hand panel tells you how many credits you have left and when they expire. It also has a link to the 'my records' tab (which is covered in Chapter 7) and interestingly a link to the previous searches that you have made. I understand that 'my searches' will become a separate tab on the 'my records' page, but that the functionality will not change.

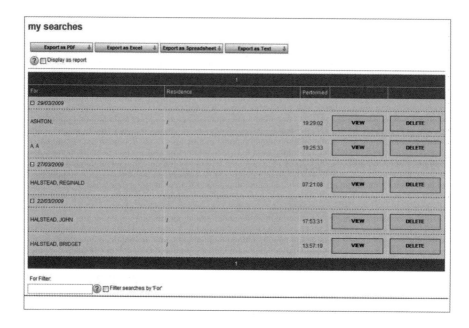

Figure 2-6 The my searches page

The result will look similar to the one above and you can view again any of the searches that it has saved for you. If you don't want to retain a specific search then the link on the right will delete it permanently.

The bottom of the screen provides a filter option so that you can check all your previous searches to see if you have been there before. Enter the name that you are interested in and then click in the little box to the right. The list will then change to those entries that contain just that name. To return to the normal view remove the filter by clicking in the box to the right again to remove the tick.

This method enables you to check quickly whether you have already searched for a particular entry rather than having to scroll through page after page.

CHAPTER 3
The person search

There is no doubt that this search is going to be the most used on the website. As you can see from the image overleaf it is split into two with the person and place searches being different so we will look at the person search in this chapter and the place search in Chapter 4. But first a few general comments before we look at the specific fields in which you can enter data.

Wildcards

As with all search engines the use of wildcards varies, so one of the first things to clarify is the use of wildcards within the site. One of the unique features of findmypast.com and 1911census.co.uk is the ability to be able to use a wildcard anywhere within a field, even at the beginning of a field rather than in the middle or end. This can be especially useful in names that commonly have a mis-spelling at the beginning – quite often last names that begin with a vowel fall into this category. But what is a wildcard? Well there are two options

The question mark '?'

This can be used to replace a single character. This can be useful if you are looking for a name with a spelling variation that involves only one change

of letter. For example B?rd, will return results for both Bird and Byrd and will find Bard as well.

The asterisk '*'

You can use an asterisk * to represent any number of characters, even a character that may or may not be there. Thus 'Hal*stead' will find Halstead and Hallstead.

We all know the confusion of looking for names that start Mc or Mac, and how interchangeable they can be with our ancestors. So using an '*' wildcard can solve the problem. Thus, M*cDonald will find both McDonald and MacDonald. Also *Donald will also find those who have been wrongly indexed with a surname of Donald and a middle name of Mc or Mac.

Do use wildcards sparingly though as they can sometimes produce unexpected results. My one-name study of Fosker has an alternative of Foskew but I can't use Foske* to find them as it will also find the much more common name Foskett as well.

Whilst we have looked at last names in the above examples you can also use a wildcard in other fields. The * may also be of use in fields, such as occupation. A search using the term *smith, will identify all the different kinds of smith. Thus *smith may return the following kinds of smith: Britannia metal smith, saw smith, boiler smith, blacksmith, shoeing smith, white smith, angle iron smith, welder and tin smith.

Although the wildcard search can greatly increase your chances of finding your ancestors, even if you are unsure as to how they spelled their name, it can also be counter productive as too much information can mask the truth. Also wildcards can only be used in certain fields, and with names only in the "advanced search".

Basic principles

The basic principle of all searching is to start with the minimum amount of information and refine the result by adding more information bit by bit. Also remember that what you think something should be is not always what was written on the census return. A typical case is my great great grandfather John Smith who was the shoemaker in Lavenham all his life, except in one census when he was down as a cordwainer.

Over the next few pages we will look at the person search screen and explain what can and cannot be done field by field.

The basic person search

The first point to make is that, at the time of writing, you must enter either a first name or a last name. You cannot leave both fields blank. This may possibly change in the future, so keep an eye on the blog on the website.

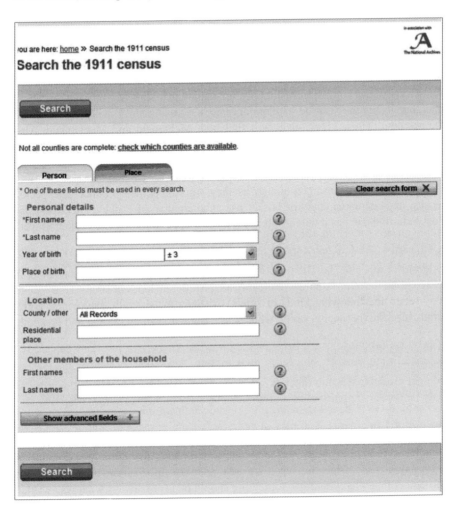

Figure 3-1 The basic person search screen

You will also notice that at the end of each line there is a question mark. If you click on this question mark then the screen is redrawn, without the loss of anything that you have entered, and helpful information relative to the field is displayed. The one shown below is the help box for the first names field.

Personal details			
*First names			(?)
*Last name	B?RD		(?)
Year of birth	1871	± 3	(?)
Place of birth			(?)
Location			
County / other	Essex		(?)
Residential place			(?)

First name ✗

Please bear in mind that on the census first names are not always spelt correctly, or in the manner you might expect.

If your initial search does not yield the relevant results then please try a variants or wildcards search. Where recorded, middle names have been included in the first name field.

PERSONAL DETAILS

This relates to what you know about the person that you are looking for.

First name

Here you can only enter a first name – you cannot use wildcards. If you wish to use a wildcard in the first name then you have to use the advanced search covered later in this chapter. So you are restricted to full names. However if you search for John (for example) it will return all entries for that name such as 'John', 'Arthur John' and 'John Arthur'. You can of course leave the first name field blank, so long as you enter a surname.

As you are probably aware from the earlier censuses many institutions entered the names of their inmates simply by their initials. For instance back in 1861 Folds Cronshaw, who was in Dartmoor Prison at the time, was down as 'F C' – he was found by looking for his initials and a place of birth which was given in full. Very rarely in the 1911 have I seen an entry, outside an institution, that has just an initial instead of a first name. You may of course see them in place of middle names. So the 'John Arthur' above becomes 'John A'

Last name

Because of the comments made earlier you are restricted to entering a full surname, if you haven't entered a first name that is. Searching just on a surname is often the first port of call for those undertaking one-name studies, so as to gather all of the entries for a name.

You can also search using just a single letter in the surname field which often finds those in an institution. There are, for example, at present 289 people with the initials 'A A'. There is also the odd anomaly. For instance there is a "Louisa A Ashton M A' in Bow who is indexed as 'Louisa A' in the first name field and 'Ashton M A' as her last name.

Year of birth and age range

One advantage of this census over all the previous ones is that it doesn't suffer from the problems of check marks all over the age column, due to the manner in which the information was collated. Because of this there should be much less chance of error.

However, it is only as good as the information entered by the person completing the return. We all, I am sure, have stories that we can tell of how 'generous' ancestors were when it came to recording their ages. Although it could just be a slip of the memory, after all how many of us get the ages of our nearest and dearest wrong!

It is also worth bearing in mind that the age may appear to be a year out. By this I mean that someone born in June 1877, who would have been 33 on the census night in April 1911, will have a computed year of birth of 1878. This is not a problem if you use a plus or minus 1 year search as it will still be found. However if you use exact year of birth then it may be that your ancestor will not be found. In these circumstances try it for the year before or the year after.

Place of birth

Another of the bones of contention that I would like to take up with my ancestors is their inability to be consistent about their place of birth. The 1911 is no different from previous censuses in this respect. However you can stumble on some real gems that may prove the breakthrough in your research. I knew from previous censuses that my wife's great grandfather was born in Ireland (I have in fact got his birth certificate as his father was in the army there in 1850) but the 1911 census entry shows his place of birth as 'British Army, Lex Killcany Ireland'.

In terms of what you can enter here you are restricted to complete place names at the moment and cannot use wildcards. Hopefully that may well change in the future. That doesn't mean though that the search engine is not flexible. If you know that your ancestor was born in Mile End, London and can't find them using that try just the word 'Mile'. Searching for the surname Antcliff and place of birth of 'Mile' reveals just one entry.

Many people are frightened of putting so little information in for fear of generating too many entries. The results cost you nothing at this stage and, should there be too many, you can always refine the search by adding more information.

One of the points that I mentioned in Chapter 2, and which is shown in the example images in Chapter 6, is that a code was added to every place of birth. A list of these codes is part of the 'about the 1911 census' section, mentioned in Chapter 2 and can be found at www.1911census.co.uk/content/default.aspx?r=24&128.

My wife's grandmother Lily Antcliff was born in Enfield, Middlesex which, according to the image, has a code of 245. Now the problem with Lily is that the last name was mis-transcribed as Autcliff and took a while to find as she wasn't with the rest of the family. So a search for Lily, with the appropriate code in the place of birth field rather than the place name may find more than just searching for the place name. It may also resolve any mis-spelling of the place of birth. Do bear in mind though that some of these codes cover very large areas. Occasionally I have seen entries where there is no code, but in these cases they are normally living in the place where they were born.

LOCATION DETAILS

This relates to what you know about where your ancestor was living or where you expect to find them.

County/other

As has been said earlier, not all of the census places are there at the minute so you need to check to make sure that the area you need is online. You will notice that there is a downward pointing arrow at the end of this field. This means that there is a pre-filled list available for you to select from.

This is the start of this list at the time of writing and as you can see it clearly marks which counties are still to be loaded. You also need to be wary when selecting a county as the counties then don't necessarily match the counties now. For example West Ham and Barking, which are now part of East London, were then part of Essex. You need also to be wary of the county boundary changes that took place in 1974. Details of most of these can be found in the relevant county pages on the Genealogy UK and Ireland website www.genuki.org.uk

You can only select one county at a time so if you are unsure which you will have to check them one at a time.

Residential place

This is the place where they were actually living. Now if this is a small village in rural Buckinghamshire you shouldn't have too many problems.

But, like the 'place of birth' field, it cannot include a wildcard which can make searching in the larger towns a lot more difficult. One way is to use the advanced search, which we will cover later. However you can be a lot more adventurous than just a place name. You can in fact enter a street name. So if you have an address, say for the birth of a child around the time of the census, you can search for 'smith' in 'mile end road' and hopefully they won't have moved! This will probably be a lot more successful than just looking for 'smith' in 'mile end'. Or you can even do something like:

First name = grace Last name = Pryer Residential place 74 markfield

This field can, in fact, contain any complete words from the following: "address, locality name, institution name, vessel name, parish name, street name, registration sub-district name, registration district name, and registration county name". So the sky is the limit as they say.

Other people living in the same household - first names and last names

These two fields let you add the details of another person who was living in the same household. It can be most helpful when searching for common names and there are too many results. So adding the details of someone else can dramatically reduce the number of results. However the first name and last name do not need to be for the same person, you can use the first name of one and the last name of another.

A word of warning – you need to be sure that the person was at the address on the night of the census, or it will be of no use. The name of this person will not appear in the result as it is simply acting as an additional filter. You can always try and 'prove' your results list by doing the search the other way round and comparing the results

One interesting statistic from the website is that 'Around 1.1% of people in the 1911 census were visitors, and around 4% were boarders'.

The advanced search

Just because you find a number of answers that seem to 'fit the bill' you don't necessarily have to pay to view them all. If the basic search doesn't give enough information for you to be sure then you may need to use the advanced search features. This is shown/hidden using the toggle button at the bottom of the screen.

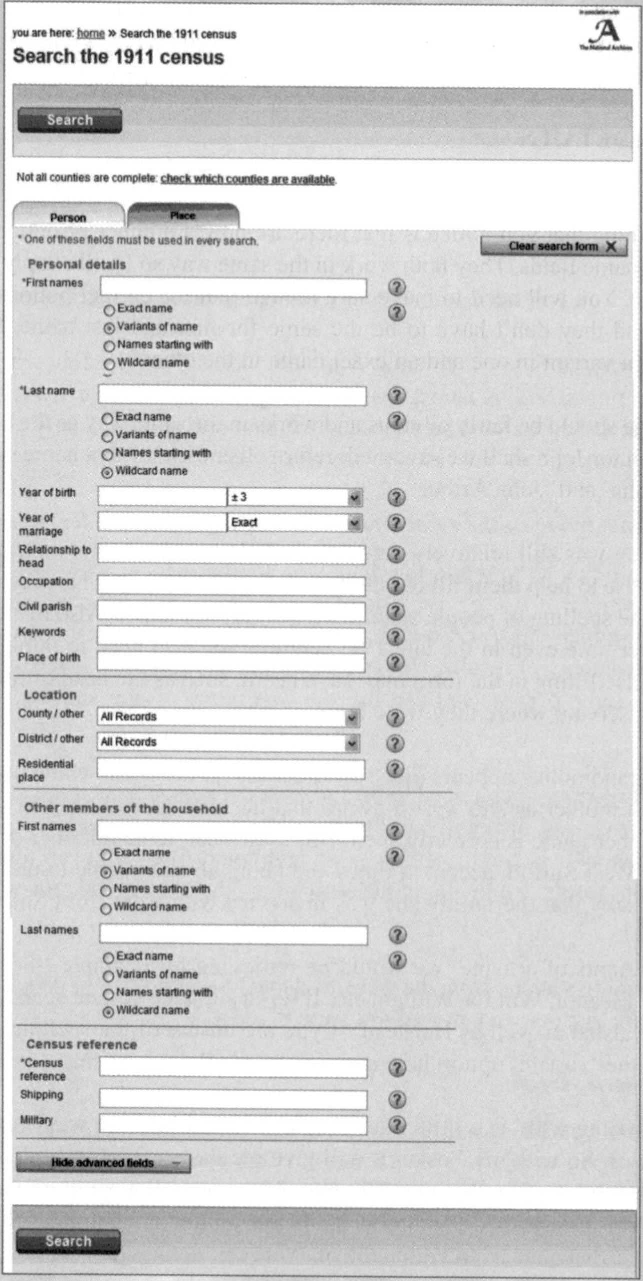

Search the 1911 census

Search

Not all counties are complete: check which counties are available.

| Person | Place |

*One of these fields must be used in every search.   Clear search form ✕

Personal details

First names
- ○ Exact name
- ◉ Variants of name
- ○ Names starting with
- ○ Wildcard name

Last name
- ○ Exact name
- ○ Variants of name
- ○ Names starting with
- ◉ Wildcard name

Year of birth   ± 3

Year of marriage   Exact

Relationship to head

Occupation

Civil parish

Keywords

Place of birth

Location

County / other   All Records

District / other   All Records

Residential place

Other members of the household

First names
- ○ Exact name
- ◉ Variants of name
- ○ Names starting with
- ○ Wildcard name

Last names
- ○ Exact name
- ○ Variants of name
- ○ Names starting with
- ◉ Wildcard name

Census reference

*Census reference

Shipping

Military

Hide advanced fields

Search

Figure 3-2 The advanced person search screen

22

I do not intend to discuss every field if the use of it is the same as in the basic search above. However one advantage of using the advanced search is that a wildcard can be used in any text-based field, that is, one without a drop-down list.

PERSON DETAILS

First and last name

The first thing that you notice is that there are now a number of options available with both name fields. They both work in the same way so I will simply explain the two in one. You will need to make sure though that the correct buttons have been selected and they don't have to be the same for first and last name. So you can search for a variant in one and an exact name in the other.

Exact name should be fairly obvious and works in the same way as the basic search. So a search for John shall we say it will return all entries for that name such as John, 'Arthur John' and 'John Arthur'.

As illiteracy was still relatively common in 1911, your ancestors may have asked someone else to help them fill out the census forms for them. This may well lead to errors in the spelling of people's names, especially surnames. Also names tended to evolve over time even in the late 19th century. You also need to think about what someone else filling in the form may have heard, such as the head of the household asking the servant where they were born.

My own grandmother appears in the 1911 census (as a servant which was a surprise to my own mother as she wasn't aware that her mother had been in service) and thankfully her name is correctly spelt. But even I can remember her dropping into her broad West Suffolk accent at times and being almost unable to understand her. She was lucky that the family she was in service with were from Suffolk as well.

So for 'variants of a name' we would be retrieving for example Ellen for Helen, Elinor for Eleanor, Wm for William etc. If it is a surname variant search then it will look for Halsted as well as Halstead. If you are unsure of the spelling of a variant name use the 'variant' option here and it will list all the ones that it is aware of.

'Names starting with' is a little like using a wildcard in some ways but it can still have its uses. So with my Fosker it will give me Fasker, Fisker, Foskett – so back to the drawing board on that one. But hopefully you will have more luck than me. Do be aware though that it will almost always produce more results but may just include one that you hadn't thought of. You can always use some of the other options to reduce the number of entries.

If you wish to use wildcards in the name searches then you will need to ensure that the last button is selected. We discussed them at the beginning of this chapter but didn't mention the use of multiple wildcards (using more than one wildcard in the same word, in this case a name but it could just as easily be a place name). This can be extremely powerful but will, if you aren't careful, generate a lot more entries than you expect.

A good example of this is the last name Randall which has many options. So using R*nd*l* will find them all, hopefully! It will produce a list of over 25,000 if used on its own so you will need to use some other search field as well. It will at least find Randle, Rendle, Randale, Rendale, Randall, Rendall, Randal, Rendal, Rundle and so on. Using the wildcard option may just find that transcription error that isn't a known variant of the name. Use it as an example to play with.

Year of birth and age range

This is the same as the basic search.

Year of marriage and range

This may be helpful with the more common names but bear in mind that it should only be recorded against a woman and if she is a widow it should not be there at all. It can often lead to 'false positives' and is something that I try to avoid using.

Relationship to the head

This is where some of the fun can start. We have all, I am sure, come across entries in previous censuses where the wife is the first person in the household (husband missing) and is listed as Wife rather than Head – the 1911 is no different. The obvious ones are easy, head, wife, son, daughter, mother, father and so on. It is when you get into the in-laws that the trouble begins. Is it down as son-in-law or 'daughters husband'? Another of the common ones is a 'step-son' being shown simply as a son, even though the surname is different.

I was recently given sight of a list of some 62,000 different relationships so far found in the 1911. Well over half of these only occurred once. I know that the team behind the census transcription is looking at ways of trying to 'link' these to a more standard version of the relationship. There are of course the odd ones that make one pause to think "My wife is his aunt" or "Boarder and uncle of the following"

However I personally prefer not to use this in a search, as I am never sure what some of my ancestors may have called themselves in relation to the other members of the household.

A case in point is that of my great grandfather Francis William Apperly. In the 1911 census as well as his family he had living with him his brother Ebor, described by him as a 'Boarder', and his sister Amelia Ellen Apperly (as Ellen Amelia) described as a 'Visitor'.

Occupation

Like relationship, this is a question at times of trying to second-guess what our ancestors may have entered. For this reason it should be one of those fields that you leave blank. If what you enter doesn't match exactly then you may end up not finding the entries you are seeking.

If you have too many results, use it with care to refine a search but don't just take the first one on the new list.

One thing that I mentioned in Chapter 2, and is shown in the example images in Chapter 6, is that a code was added to every occupation rather than them being crossed through as in previous censuses.

You can in fact search on these codes. A list of the major codes can be found in the 'about the 1911 census' page or at www.1911census.co.uk/content/default.aspx?r=24&127. You can also search for more than one word so you can look for 'ship carpenter' as opposed to 'house carpenter' rather than just a carpenter. Each of these will give fewer entries than looking at the codes 210 or 211.

Another of the interesting statistics from the site is that 'that around 30% of women did not give an occupation'.

Civil parish

To quote from the website "A civil parish is a small-scale unit of local government and is distinct from an Ecclesiastical Parish, whose boundaries were determined by the Church. In size, it is the next census geographical unit (of any value to the family historian) down from a registration sub-district." It can be useful if you are searching for a very common name in a large place like London but you will need to know exactly how it has been spelt or used.

Keywords

Unless you already know of the person's existence in the census and know the correct keyword it doesn't always work the way that you might expect. According to the online help the 'Keyword' field looks very specifically at the following fields from the census return: 'rank, unit of arm of service, rank or rating or branch of service, marital status, industry or service to which a worker was connected, whether an employer, a working or working on their own account, nationality, language spoken, vessel name, and institution name.'

Place of birth

Is exactly the same as described in the basic search.

LOCATION DETAILS

County/others

This is exactly the same as described in the basic search.

District/other

This is another drop-down list already populated with the complete list of Registration districts. You can find details of registration districts within the relevant county pages of the Genuki site www.genuki.org.uk.

If you select a county from the county list then only those districts relative to that county are included. You will need to be careful though as no doubt you are aware that some districts straddle county boundaries.

Residential place

This is the same as in the basic search.

Other members of the household

Again the comments are the same as the basic search but with the added possibility of being able to use the filter options described at the start of this description of the advanced search.

Census reference

If you know the reference to a specific page then you can use this field to go straight to that page. The references are quite lengthy when compared with the previous censuses and are explained in chapter 6.

THE RESULTS

Having entered your search details and initiated the search, what are you going to get? If your search returns too many entries you will get a screen like the following which was the result of looking for all John Smith's.

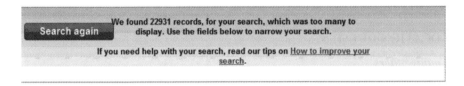

If we redefine this to look at those simply in London then the result of the search is:

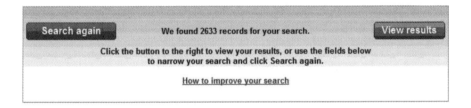

Here we have the option to view the records at 30 entries to the page (at present) and page through them if we wish or we can refine the search further.

If on the other hand the number of entries is below 1,000 (present level – it may well change) then the results will be displayed and look like this result from the search for John Halstead.

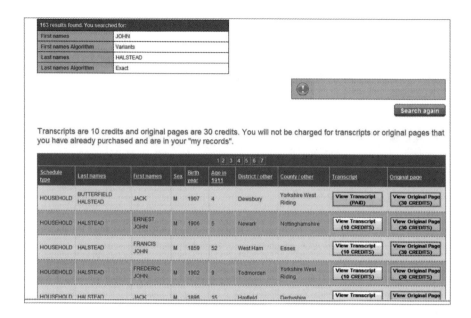

Figure 3-3 The person search result

You can go back to refine the search at any time by using the 'search again' button which stays on the top of every page.

The top box shows you exactly what you have searched for so there is no confusion - in this case, variants of John as a first name and the exact last name Halstead. If I changed the search and looked for an exact first name of John and a last name as variants of Halstead then I will get 178 results instead of 163.

Obviously the more complex the search the more information will be included as this one for John Smith shows.

28

Because there are more than 30 results for John Halstead there are multiple pages and you can page through them using the page links in the top blue line of the results.

This shows that we are currently on page 1 – it changes as you view the different pages.

You may also just be able to see – but I have blown it up here – that each of the headings is underlined. They are in fact hyperlinks and clicking on any one of them will sort the results on that column. If it is a name field then it will be sorted in alphabetical order from A-Z, if the age column, then it will sort into age order starting with the youngest. The birth year will sort into chronological order. If you click the same heading again then it will reverse the order so that the alpha based fields become sorted from Z-A. Sorting the birth year a second time will give the most recent first.

You will notice in the name column the point I made earlier about the first names where John has been included even as a middle name. The result also states in the first column whether the entry was found in a household, institutional or military schedule.

The result does not list by town or village but registration district instead. This can make it a little more challenging if you have a lot of people with the same name in the same area. Of the 163 John Halstead's 34 of them are in the Burnley Registration District. I can of course refine the list by using things like place of birth and age, but I am still likely to be left with more than one.

If the result is for just a surname then you may think that sorting into District order may help. The answer is - Not necessarily! A lot will depend on how common that name is in that area. You also need to bear in mind that there may be more than one household of that name.

CHAPTER 4

The place search

A s you can see, the place search is a lot simpler than the person search. I suppose, to be more accurate, it ought to be called an address search as you have to provide a street name.

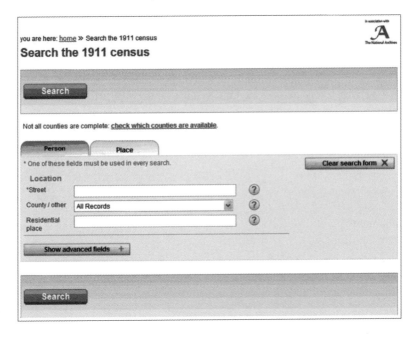

Figure 4-1 The basic place search screen

Like the person search, let's look at the fields one by one.

Street name

You have to enter a street name or part of one. You do not need to enter house numbers or names or any other part of the address. So you enter just 'Mile End Road' or is it 'Mile End Rd' or any other combination! So to be on the safe side we can enter just 'Mile End' except that there are 7,581of them and it asks you to refine the search. I tried it with a couple of the roads in the village where I live and it gave almost no results yet most of them were certainly there at the time.

County/other

This is the same as in the person search.

Residential place

Again this is the same as the person search.

I found it frustrating trying to find some of the addresses that I knew of. And even a simple task like finding the place my great great grandfather Henry Noyce lived in at the time of the 1881 census was fraught with problems. It was Henry who caused my real interest in the census when I found him transcribed in the original CD-Rom version of the 1881 census as Henry Nogee.

In those days (the late 1990's) there were no easy ways of searching, certainly not in places like London, especially if you had no idea where they were. In Henry's case he was living at 118 Asylum Road, Camberwell and the house still exists today.

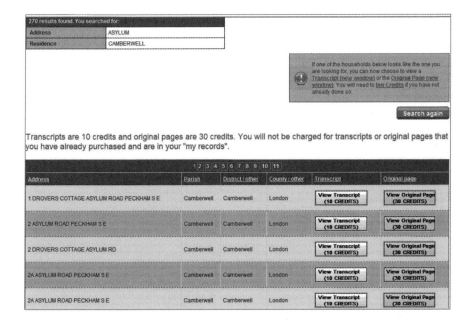

Figure 4-2 The result of a search for Asylum Road in Camberwell

This is the start of the list of some 270 households with the name Asylum in the street name within Camberwell. We can see at the bottom that there are two households for 2a Asylum Road. Now if you knew that your ancestor lived there which one would you take? You could be even more unlucky and find that there are several households within a property.

The answer is to go back to the person search, enter the surname that you are interested in and enter the address '2a Asylum road' as the 'Residential place'.

Be aware that over time some streets have changed their names. For example Albert Road, Peckham was changed to Consort Road as there were too many streets with that name in London.

Now whilst the help for the address says that you shouldn't include the street number at the time of writing it certainly works if you enter it. Mind that is not to say that it still will in the future! Also be aware that just as some streets changed their names, some buildings changed their street number.

If you want to view the household transcription or the image then just click on the appropriate icon in the listing and you will then see the relevant image. Details of transcriptions and images can be found in chapter 6.

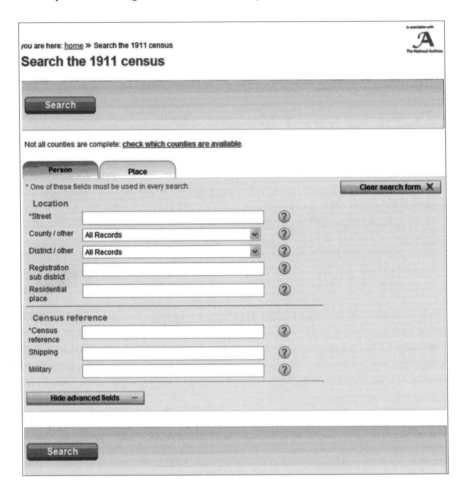

Figure 4-3 The advanced place search screen

The advanced search doesn't make it any easier. The additional fields that are added are the same as those added in the advanced person search.

District / other and **Census references**

Registration sub district

This one is new but in some ways if you know this then you will already have found the answer to the question!

There is some helpful information on the website under 'Place search' in the 'help & advice' section which might explain some of the problems.

"The source of the address details on the 1911 census is the original form filled in by the householder, and several factors conspire to make finding an address (from the information provided in the historical document) difficult:

In 1911, the concept of a full postal address with a number and street was less evolved than it is today. Many people listed their address as a house name followed by a town (rather than a house number and street name) and this was the information that was transcribed.

Only a small space was left on the original form for the address, and the householder would often further abbreviate the address to make it fit.

Many householders also used abbreviations for phrases (as we do today), such as 'Rd' for 'Road'.

Place names and spellings may have changed over time. For example Pixham Lane in Dorking was also entered by householders as Pixholme in a number of instances."

"To help resolve these issues we are working on a number of ways to make finding an address simpler:

We will be applying data enhancements and standardisation over the coming months to try to smooth over common inconsistencies in the original documents, so that when you enter terms such as 'Acacia Avenue', for example, it will return all the instances of 'Acacia Ave' as well.

We will soon release the enumerators' original books, which list the households and heads in each area. This information could be used to identify neighbouring houses when the address information left by our ancestors makes this hard to recover. If you have already paid to view one household image in a particular street, you will be able to view the linked Enumerators' book images for free, by returning to your saved records and then clicking a link to the images. You will not be required to make further payment to view these.

We will also be adding a wildcard search to the street field to allow you to search laterally."

"It may also help to do the following as part of your search:

Check old maps online and other sources to discover whether names have changed, or have more than one spelling.

Search for common alternative spellings, such as 'ham' for 'holme' and vice versa; for example Pixham and Pixholme

Search for 'St' as well as 'Street', 'Road' and 'Rd', 'Avenue' and 'Ave', and 'Ln' in addition to 'Lane', etc, or miss these Suffixes off entirely. For example, Wessenden instead of Wessenden Road."

It can only get better.

CHAPTER 5
Registration and Payments

I t is likely to be the end of 2009 before a subscription facility will be available for the 1911 and therefore the pay-per-view option is the only one available at present.

Therefore, in order to look at any transcriptions or images, you need to buy some credits or, if you are already registered with the sister site www.findmypast.com and have credits there, you can use those on the 1911 site. If you already have a subscription with findmypast.com then you will still need to buy credits but you can use your usual sign-in on the 1911 website.

There are a number of ways that you can get to the Register/Sign-in screen shown below - from the sign-in or register links on the top of the screen, by clicking on a link to look at a transcription or image (if you aren't already signed in) or from the 'buy credits' link (again if you aren't already signed in).

Whichever option you use you will end up at the following screen.

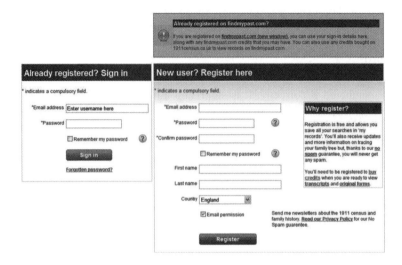

Figure 5-1 Registration and sign-in screen

Sign in

If you already have an account with findmypast.com or the 1911census then simply enter your email address and password in the appropriate places on the left.

One word of warning though – if you are likely to use the account away from your home (at a local library or somewhere like the Society of Genealogists) then please make sure that you read the warning later under "My Account".

REGISTER

If you are new to either site or if you want a separate account for your pay-per-view from your subscription account then you will need to complete the section on the right. Note: **The top three fields are mandatory.**

Email address

The email address must be unique – that is if you are trying to create a separate account for pay-per-view or want a different account to your partner – then you will need a different email address. These days that should not be a problem as most Internet Service Providers (ISPs) let you have more than one for any account. If you try to use an email address that is already in use you will be told to use a different one.

The email address should also be a valid one as it will be used to provide feed back from either the 1911census.com or findmypast.com management, whether it be to tell you of the latest changes to the site, send you details of a forgotten password or the acknowledgement of a correction that you have submitted.

Passwords

You are asked to enter a password twice. The reason for this is to ensure that you have remembered it correctly. It is surprising how many people can't remember their passwords these days. For the best security, and after all it is there to protect your investment, it should ideally be a combination of lowercase and uppercase letters and numbers. Try to stay away from passwords that are easily guessable such as your mother's maiden name or your date of birth. You can change your password at any time using the 'my account' link at the top of the screen.

Whether you tick the box for the system to remember your password is up to you. If you are only using the account at home then it should not be a problem. However, if you use it in a public place, such as a library, then you might want to leave it blank and enter the password each time. If you tell it to remember then anyone else using the 1911census on that machine and clicking the 'sign-in' link will sign in as you and can easily use all your credits. If this should happen then there is nothing that you can do about it. It will be deemed your fault for leaving your password on an open system.

You have the chance to enter the details of your name here. It is used to create the "Welcome back ... (your name)" text when you sign in and it is also used in email correspondence from either site.

Forgotten password

If you forget your password then you can click on the link below the 'sign-in' details and you will be presented with the following screen.

Figure 5-2 Forgotten password screen

You simply enter your email address, click on the submit button and a new one will be sent to you. These are normally letter and number strings that aren't easily remembered, but you can use the 'my account' screen to change it.

MY ACCOUNT

If at any time you want to amend your details, then once you are signed in, you can use the 'my account' link in the top of the screen or the 'update your profile' beside the welcome back message. This will display the 'update my profile' screen.

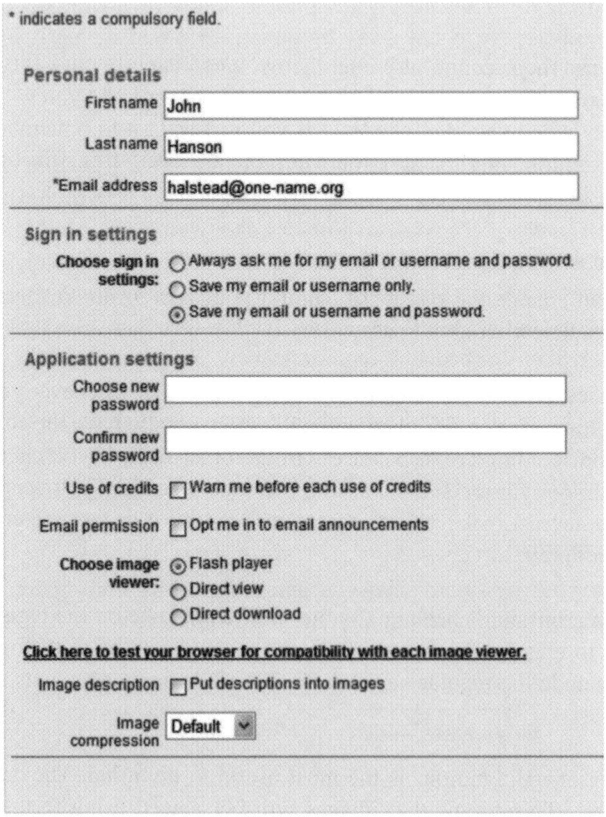

* indicates a compulsory field.

Personal details

First name |John

Last name |Hanson

*Email address |halstead@one-name.org

Sign in settings

Choose sign in settings: ○ Always ask me for my email or username and password.
○ Save my email or username only.
⦿ Save my email or username and password.

Application settings

Choose new password |

Confirm new password |

Use of credits ☐ Warn me before each use of credits

Email permission ☐ Opt me in to email announcements

Choose image viewer: ⦿ Flash player
○ Direct view
○ Direct download

Click here to test your browser for compatibility with each image viewer.

Image description ☐ Put descriptions into images

Image compression |Default ▾|

Figure 5-3 My account screen

Personal details

The first and last names we have covered before in this chapter but you can change them if you want to. Should you need to change your email address this is possible.

You don't need to create a new account when you change ISP just update the existing email address with the new one. A word of warning though – it will take whatever you enter and not even ask for confirmation that it is correct, so type carefully and check it.

Sign in settings

Here you choose which of the options about the 'sign in' screen best suits your needs. Because these are 'radio buttons' one of them will always be selected and it should show the one that is currently active. In this case it is set to remember my details.

If you only use the account 'at home' then you can happily click this last icon and it will remember both your e-mail address and password and you will be signed in automatically when you click the link. If you just want it to remember the user ID then use the middle button and if you want it to ask every time (the option to select if you use it in public places) then use the top button.

Application settings

Here you can change the password, should you wish to do so. Bear in mind the comments made earlier about passwords.

The first check box is 'use of credits'. If left blank then whenever you click a link to look at a transcription or image you will automatically have the charge deducted from your outstanding credit balance. On the other hand if you check the box, as shown, then you will receive a warning message whenever you want to view one. This should at least make you re-check that you have in fact selected the correct image/transcription to view.

The 'email permission' check box is the same as the one on the registration screen and relates to email announcements from the 1911 site or from findmypast.com. This will include the regular newsletters as well as announcements about changes on either site.

The next set of radio buttons is the most useful to my mind. The default is to use 'flash player'. This means that images will be viewed using to the Adobe Flash plug-in Viewer that is installed in most machines.

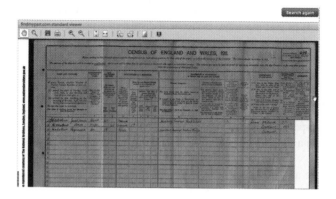

Figure 5-4 An image viewed with the Adobe Flash plug-in viewer

This displays the image in the same window as part of the normal viewer. The line of icons above the image gives you the ability to zoom in or out, rotate the image if it is upside down as well as print and save the image.

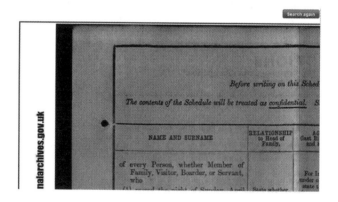

Figure 5-5 An image viewed with the normal viewer

By selecting the middle option of 'direct view' you have a much larger image to start with but there are no controls and you can only save the image to a file by 'right clicking' it, as one would save any other image on a website to a file on your PC hard drive.

Both of the above images are of the same area of the screen viewing the same image.

The third option 'direct download', and the one that I use, gives you the option the image or save it to you machine. Either will display the image in a separate window using the default viewer for your machine for JPG images. This means that you can view the original transcription at the same time. There is nothing worse than having going backwards and forwards between image and transcription to check them.

HOW TO PAY

As this is a pay-per-view site there are two ways of paying. You can either use vouchers (more of this in a minute) or you can purchase a PayAsYouGo credit package.

Currently there are three credits options:

◆ £6.95 for 60 credits which expire in 90 days
◆ £24.95 for 280 credits which expire in 365 days
◆ £49.95 for 600 credits which expire in 365 days

These credits are also useable on the main Findmypast.com website. If you get to the stage that your time has nearly expired but you haven't used them all you can top them up with a minimum payment and it will extend the life of them all by 90 days.

Selecting the 'buy credits' option from the top of the screen will take you to the following screen.

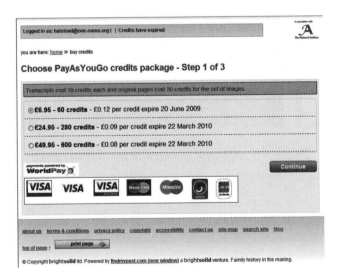

Figure 5-6 Paying for credits

Once you have selected the package that you wish to purchase click the continue button and you will be taken to the Worldpay secure payment page.

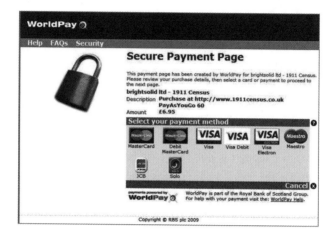

Figure 5-7 Secure payment screen

Select the method that you wish to pay by and you will be taken to the screen to enter your credit or debit card details. These are perfectly secure websites so you need have no fears. You will be sent a confirmation email to prove your purchase and your credits will appear immediately on your account. If for some reason this doesn't happen refresh your screen (usually the F5 function key). If that doesn't work try signing out and then back in again and if that fails contact the Customer Support team (their details are on the website under – Contact us) and they will need the details from your confirmation email. It might be worth checking your junk or spam emails if it doesn't arrive.

Using vouchers

If you are unhappy about using a credit card online or don't have one then the only option is to buy vouchers. These are available from many places including many libraries and details can be found on the website under the 'about vouchers' section of 'help and advice'. Vouchers are £5.00 and give 40 credits.

Figure 5-8 Front and back of voucher

Activating a voucher though is not very easy and needs to be done through the findmypast.com website and not the 1911census.co.uk site. Once you sign in there you will find a link on the home page to activate a voucher which will present this screen.

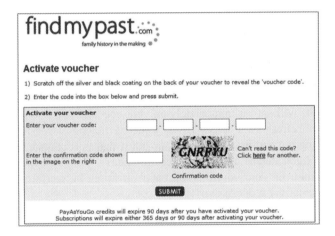

Figure 5-9 Activating a voucher

The four boxes along the top are for the code that is under the scratch panel on the back of the card. A word of warning – the codes are all alpha but 'O' is not used ('Q' is). In the box on the line below you need to enter the letters as read from the screen – they are different every time. The credits will then be added to your account. If they are not then contact the Customer Support team as above.

CHAPTER 6
Transcriptions and images explained

Looking at the transcription

As mention before, the site is not a subscription or free site and it is made quite clear above the results listing what the cost is for looking at the transcription and images.

If you are not signed in or registered then clicking either the 'view transcript' or 'view original page' for any entry will take you to the 'registration/sign-in' screen, which is described fully in Chapter 5.

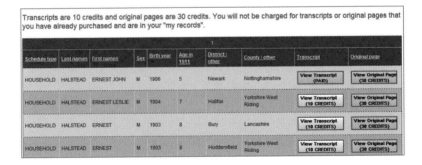

Figure 6-1 The search result

47

You will notice at the end of each line that there is an icon that will enable you to view the transcription or the image. In each case it confirms how many credits it will cost you. You will also notice that I have already looked at the entry for Ernest John Halstead. If I look at it again I will not be charged, so long as it remains in the history records within the site. (This is covered in Chapter 7). Once you have looked at a transcription or an image for a person then the rest of the people in that household are also marked as having been viewed and you can view them again for free at any time.

If you have ticked the box about the 'use of credits', in your profile, then you will see the following message asking for confirmation before the credits are deducted from your account.

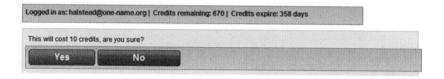

The details of the transcriptions that you will see are shown below and examples of images follow later in the chapter.

The result that you will see for a household transcription should be similar to this one for Ernest John Halstead, his parents and family.

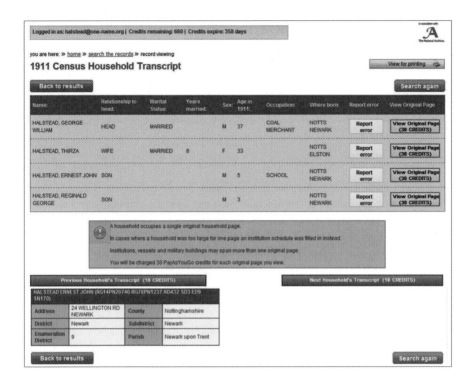

Figure 6-2 A household schedule transcript

The transcription shows everyone on the household schedule but it is not a complete transcription, as there are several pieces of information missing. What is omitted is the number of children that the couple had and how many have died, the code numbers that relate to the occupations and place of birth and the type of work (Industry or service) and whether employed or a worker. Details of these are shown in the later section on images.

You can view the next or previous household schedule within the piece by using the buttons below the transcription. In each case it will cost you 10 credits to view the transcription of that household.

If you want to view the original schedule for yourself, bearing in mind that it is likely to have been completed by the head of the household and signed by them, you need to click on the link on the right hand end of the line against any of the names.

HALSTEAD ERNEST JOHN (RG14PN20740 RG78PN1237 RD432 SD3 ED9 SN170)			
Address	24 WELLINGTON RD NEWARK	County	Nottinghamshire
District	Newark	Subdistrict	Newark
Enumeration District	9	Parish	Newark upon Trent

The last item of note on the page is the box of information at the bottom of the transcription. It is expanded here to make it easier to read. This gives all of the information about the address of the property. So this particular family was living at 24 Wellington Rd, Newark, Nottinghamshire. It is in the parish of Newark upon Trent, in the sub-district of Newark and the Registration District of Newark.

In the blue heading line is the complete reference for that schedule. The first thing that strikes one is that the reference is exceedingly long when compared with the earlier census return references. This is due mainly to the fact that it comprises the references to both the schedule and the enumerator's book that goes with it. You should really make a note of the complete reference. It can be highlighted and then you can use cut and paste to copy it wherever you want.

This particular schedule reference is made up as follows:

RG14PN20740, RG78PN1237, RD432, SD3, ED9, SN170

RG14PN20740	The piece number that the schedule comes from
RG78PN1237	The enumerators' summary book number
RD432	The Registration District number
SD3	The Registration Sub District number
ED9	The Enumeration District number
SN170	The schedule number within the piece number above

There are, as I explained in Chapter 1, a number of households are larger than the fifteen entries on a standard schedule. For these a couple of different types of schedule were used depending on the number of people in the household (up to 40 or up to 100). Places like hotels fell into this category as they aren't of course institutions.

If you find one of these then you are likely to get a result that looks like this at the bottom of the transcription.

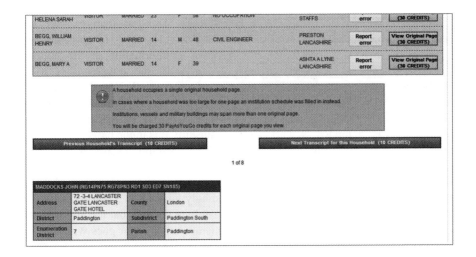

Figure 6-3 Household schedule for a large household

You will notice that it says that this is page one of eight and also that the grey button above on the right now says 'Next Transcript for this Household' rather than 'Next Household's Transcript'. Similarly as you move through the pages of this schedule 'Previous Household's Transcript' will change to 'Previous transcript for this household'. Bearing in mind that each page will cost you 10 credits. With these larger schedules the address box and signature is on the last page.

Unfortunately at the time of writing there appears to be no way of going from page one to page eight without viewing each transcription in between.

Institution transcription

1911 Census Institution Transcript   View for printing

Back to results   Search again

Name:	Age:	Sex:	Relationship:	Report error	View Original Page
HOPKINSON, STOTT	55	M	INMATE	Report error	View Original Page (30 CREDITS)
HEBDEN, JOHN	71	M	INMATE	Report error	View Original Page (30 CREDITS)
HORSFALL, SARAH ANN	36	F	INMATE	Report error	View Original Page (30 CREDITS)
HARRISON, LOUISA	63	F	INMATE	Report error	View Original Page (30 CREDITS)
HELLIWELL, ANN	63	F	INMATE	Report error	View Original Page (30 CREDITS)

Figure 6-4 An institution schedule transcript

Previous Transcript for this Institution (10 CREDITS)   Next Transcript for this Institution (10 CREDITS)

7 of 18

HALSTEAD ALBERT (RG14PN26516 RD496 SD5 ED65 SN9999)

Institution name		Halifax Union Workhouse, Gibbet Street	
Address	GIBBET STREET HALIFAX	County	Yorkshire West Riding
District	Halifax	Subdistrict	Halifax South
Enumeration District	65	Parish	Halifax

As you can see this transcription contains a lot less information than with a normal household in terms of the detail for each person. The information at the bottom of the page does tell you that this is The Union Workhouse, Gibbet St, Halifax. You will need to look at the image of course to find out more about Albert Halstead, who appears in the middle of the transcribed page.

You will also notice that it tells you that this is page 7 of the 18 that make up this particular workhouse. You can view the next and previous pages of the workhouse using the same method as view next and previous households. Unlike a household schedule there are no details of the address or signature on the bottom of the schedule, as it appears on the last page. They also contain 30 people to a page.

Military Transcription

A military transcription is the same as any other institution transcription giving the name of the barracks in place of the address. At the time of writing only information for military establishments in England are available as they are included in the county where the barracks are situated. For information relating to the army overseas, which appears for the first time in 1911, we will have to wait until the end of the project. This is because the piece numbers are included right at the very end and scanning and transcription are being done in piece number order.

Shipping transcription

The transcription for a Shipping schedule is again slightly different. This one is for the Halstead family on '86 Aire & Calder Fly Boat'.

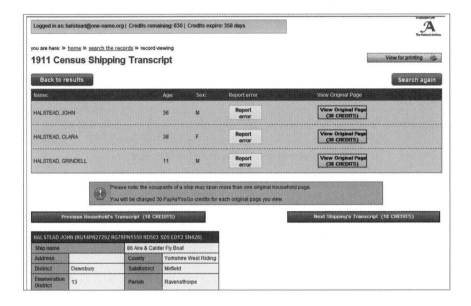

Figure 6-5 A shipping schedule transcript

At the top of each of these pages you will notice that there are three links. The one on the left '**Back to results**' will take you back to your initial search result so you can select another household to view if need be. The green one on the right '**Search Again**' will take you back to the search screen so you can refine the search if it is not correct. Finally the one above, 'View for Printing', will provide a more printer friendly version of the transcription, should you wish to print the page.

Reporting errors

No transcription process of a large number of records is ever going to be 100% accurate. The fact that with the 1911 census we are dealing with nearly 8 million sets of different handwriting makes that a certainty. There are also errors made by our ancestors in completing the forms that lead to a different type of error. These, in the older censuses, are known as enumerators' errors as it was often the enumerator, in copying the information, who was thought to be responsible for the mistake.

With these returns being in the hands of our ancestors it is quite possible that some of the errors in the earlier censuses may not have been the enumerator at all but our own ancestors in writing the information to begin with.

However, the only errors that should be reported are those that are a genuine mis-reading of what was written. The other errors are unfortunate but not ones that should be reported, they just cause us frustration in finding our ancestors. You have to remember that just because the spelling isn't what you expect it to be, it isn't necessarily an error.

Should you find a genuine transcription error, and the only way to do that is to look at the image, then you have a means of being able to report it. You will notice that there is a yellow square on every line of a transcription, just before the icon to view the image. This is there to enable you to report any errors that you might find in the transcription.

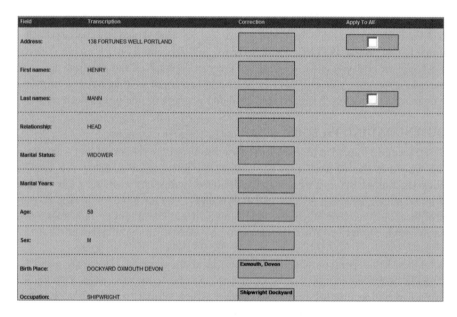

Figure 6-6 The error reporting screen

The above image is the top of the error reporting screen with the current information from the website on the left hand side and on the right a space to fill in the correct transcription. You will notice that with the householder's last name you have the ability to specify that every individual in the household with that error should be corrected, if it is incorrect.

In this particular case, as you can see from the image on the left, the error is the place of birth for Henry Mann which should read Exmouth, Devon not Oxmouth. The person writing the entry wrote with a curly capital 'E' that was common at the time. However in his case the top was almost non-existant. The word 'Dockyard' is actually in the 'whether working at home' column, which is part of the occupation data. Once you have entered all the corrections click the 'submit' button that is at the bottom of the screen.

You will be sent an email confirmation that the request has been logged and giving a reference number. Unfortunately the email does not include the details of what you have corrected so you will either need to remember or update the email with the information. Not easy when you have corrected more than one entry in a household.

Unlike findmypast.com where the errors are processed and the update posted immediately online, the error corrections are only processed once a month with the 1911 census and you have to wait for the next upload of the database for it to become apparent. You will also be sent another email at that point confirming whether the correction has been approved and is going online or has been rejected.

DOWNLOADING IMAGES

So far we have looked at indexes and transcriptions of the schedules, but what about the schedules themselves? In order to view the image of a schedule you need to click the link at the end of any transcription or index entry where it says 'View original page'. This will cost you 30 credits and if you have the box ticked in your profile about the 'use of credits' then you will get the dialogue box mentioned earlier asking you to confirm the deduction of credits from your account.

A lot then will depend on which option you use to view images. If you are using the you will be presented with a screen similar to the one on the next page. Your choice of viewer will you will be presented with a screen similar to this. Your choice of viewer will dictate the amount of flexibility that you have over manipulating the image.

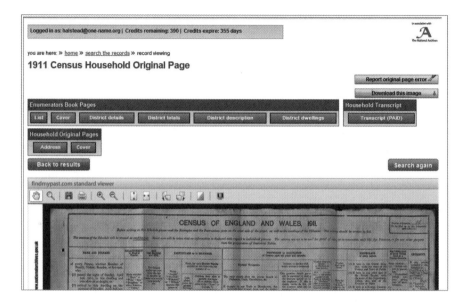

Figure 6-7 The schedule image viewed with Flash Player

If on the other hand you use the 'direct download' option which I use you will be presented with the following screen.

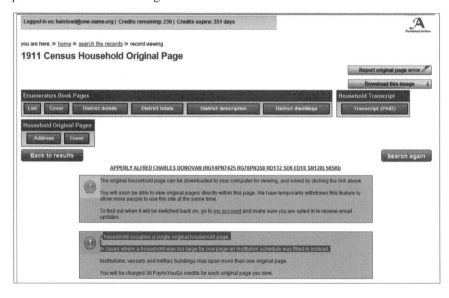

Figure 6-8 Download images screen.

From here you have two ways of downloading the image - by using the 'download this image' button at the top right of the screen or by using the hyperlink in the middle of the screen, which has the name of the person highlighted and the schedule reference.

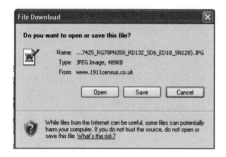

Either way the dialogue box here is displayed. You can cancel the download, save it to your hard drive or simply open it to look at.

If you open it then the file is actually downloaded to your computer but into the temporary Internet files. The file will then be opened by whichever program you have associated with viewing Jpeg images. How you manipulate the image from then on will depend upon that program. Examples of the images are later in this chapter.

If you save the file to the hard drive then the standard dialogue box used to save a file will be presented and ask you where on your computer you wish to save the file. The default file name is the name of the person from the transcribed followed by the full TNA reference. If you have ticked the 'image description' box in your profile this file name will be added to the left hand side your downloaded image. These preset file names can be quite long and you may want to just keep the schedule details rather than the name as well - you can edit the file name accordingly.

The additional pieces
The observant amongst you who may have used the site since its start will have noticed the new images that are now available. These were only introduced at the end of April 2009. They include all of the other images that have been promised since the site was first launched. Access to all of these additional images is free so long as you have looked at the image of the schedule. So the 30 credits gives you access to eight additional images. Whether the cost is worth it I will leave you to decide.

What you get are the additional images from the schedule itself comprising the cover for the piece that the schedule is part of as well as the front of the schedule which was given to the head of the household to complete. It is the reverse that we see with the details of the schedule.

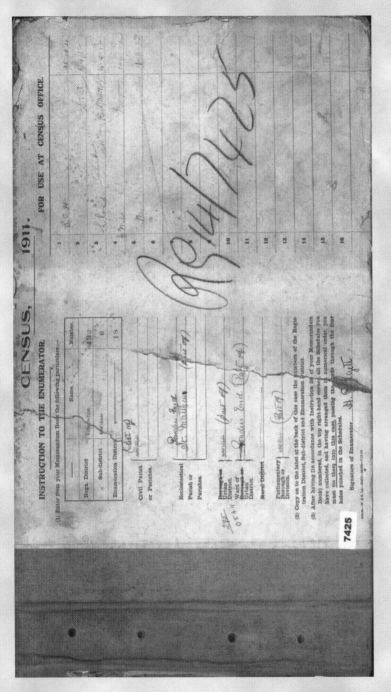

Figure 6-9 Cover of piece number RG14PN7425

This is the book that contains the details of my grandfather Alfred Charles Donovan Apperly. The left of the page contains the details of the area covered. In the days of the old style census returns this is the information that went across the top of every page. The right hand side has the details of the checkers who no doubt collated all the information that formed the statistics obtained from the census.

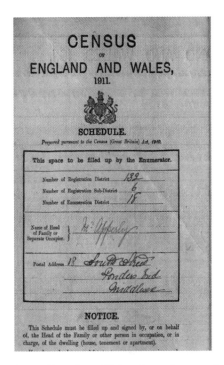

Figure 6-10 Cover of schedule for 18 South St, Ponders End

This is the cover of the schedule that was given to Mr Apperly, my great grandfather Francis William Apperly. This is actually part of the folded form that was handed to the householder and the reverse of the schedule of which it is a part is shown as figure 6-28. The image of the schedule for Francis is shown as figure 6-20.

As well as the additional two images from RG14 you get the six images from the enumerator's books (if they survived).

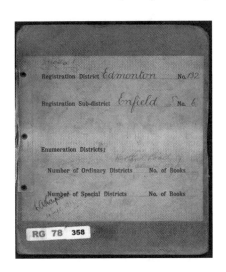

Figure 6-11 Cover of enumerators book RG78/358

This is the front cover of the book For Enfield a sub-district of Edmonton.

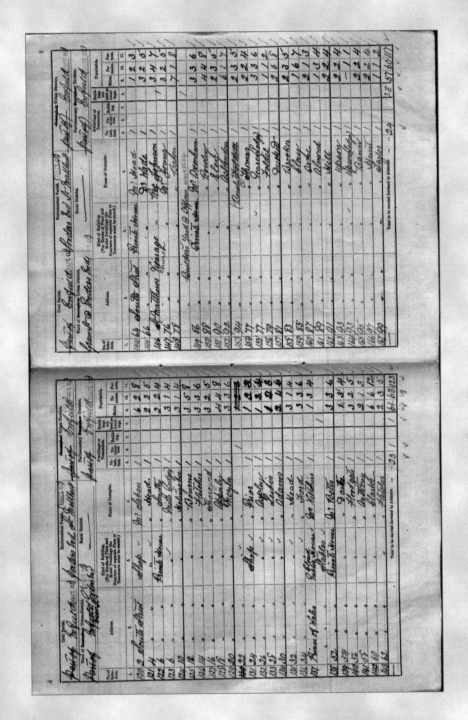

Figure 6-12 List of properties in RG14/PN7425

Figure 6-12 on page 60 shows pages 6 and 7 of the list of schedules that make up this particular piece. This page covers schedule numbers 120-167. The one for my great grandfather was number 128. This listing is a lot more informative than just a list of the names of heads of households in the adjacent houses.

It shows that houses numbered 2 and 4 were shops, no doubt with people living above them, as opposed to empty premises. House numbers 24-34 are also shops and the next property is the Princes of Wales public house (which it says is closed). Next door (but as part of the same schedule number) are some stables. The next entry of interest is the one after schedule 148 which says that there is a builders yard and offices, obviously unoccupied. So you can see that these documents tell you a lot about the neighbourhood.

At the bottom of the page are the totals of occupied and unoccupied properties as well as the total number of males and females. This information was then transferred to the page showing the totals for the District as a whole.

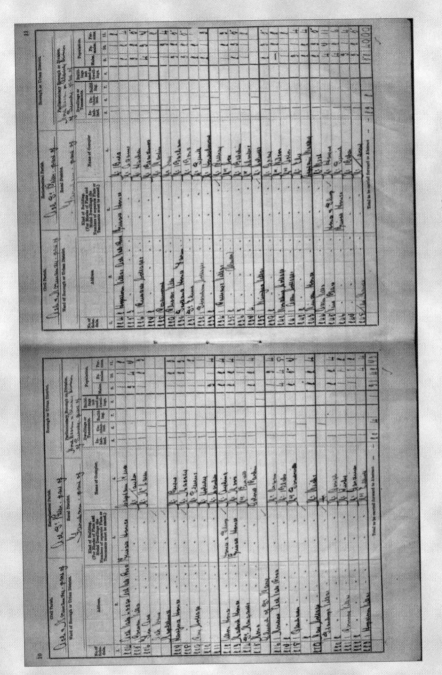

Figure 6-13 List of properties showing more than one household in a property

This list of schedules shows more than one household living at the properties in the Civil Parish of Ash & Normandy.

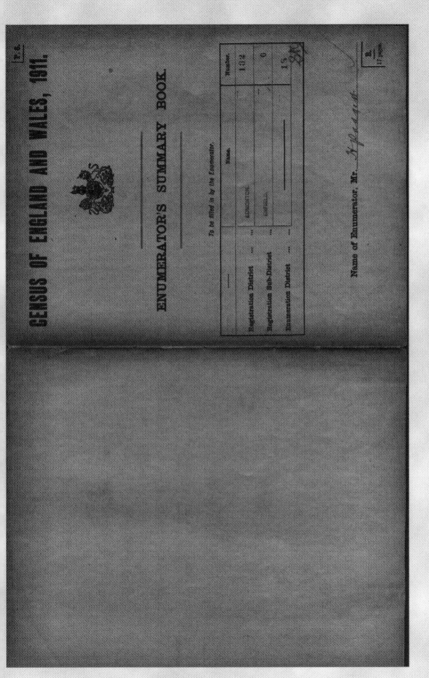

Figure 6-14 District details

This contains the details of the district.

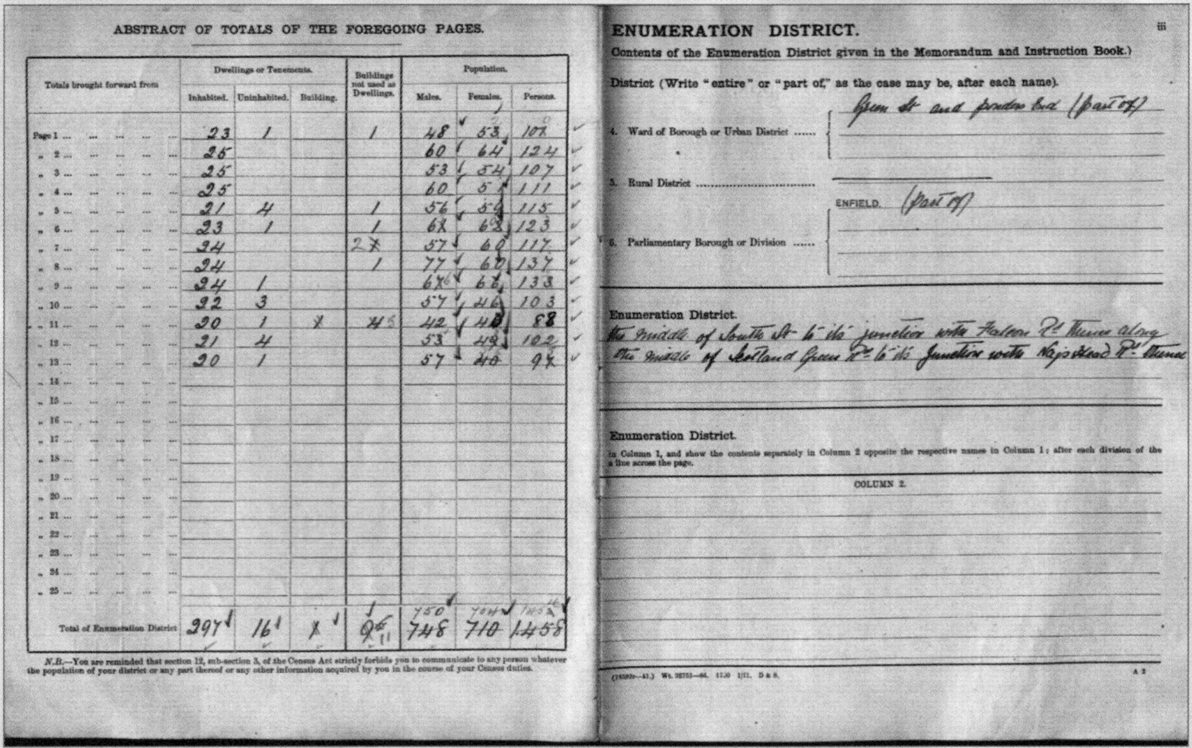
ABSTRACT OF TOTALS OF THE FOREGOING PAGES.

Totals brought forward from	Dwellings or Tenements: Inhabited.	Uninhabited.	Building.	Buildings not used as Dwellings.	Population: Males.	Females.	Persons.
Page 1	23	1		1	48	53	101
2	25				60	64	124
3	25				53	54	107
4	25				60	51	111
5	21	4		1	56	59	115
6	23	1		1	61	62	123
7	24			27	57	60	117
8	24			1	77	60	137
9	24	1			61	61	133
10	22	3			57	46	103
11	20	1	1	45	42	46	88
12	21	4			53	49	102
13	20	1			57	40	97
14							
15							
16							
17							
18							
19							
20							
21							
22							
23							
24							
25							
Total of Enumeration District	297	16	1	96	750 748	704 710	1454 1458

N.B.—You are reminded that section 12, sub-section 3, of the Census Act strictly forbids you to communicate to any person whatever the population of your district or any part thereof or any other information acquired by you in the course of your Census duties.

ENUMERATION DISTRICT. iii

Contents of the Enumeration District given in the Memorandum and Instruction Book.)

District (Write "entire" or "part of," as the case may be, after each name).

4. Ward of Borough or Urban District ...... Green St and ponders End (part of)

5. Rural District ......

6. Parliamentary Borough or Division ...... ENFIELD. (part of)

Enumeration District.

the middle of South St to its junction with Falcon Rd thence along the middle of Scotland Green Rd to its junction with Nags Head Rd thence

Enumeration District.

in Column 1, and show the contents separately in Column 2 opposite the respective names in Column 1; after each division of the a line across the page.

COLUMN 2.

(18392r—41.) Wt. 28735—66. 17.0 1/11. D & S. A 2

Figure 6-15 District totals

This is the left hand page of the two and contains the details from the bottom of each of the listing pages. It shows that this area had 313 dwellings, of which 16 were unoccupied. There was a total of 1454 people living in the area covered on census night. The page on the right is part of the district description.

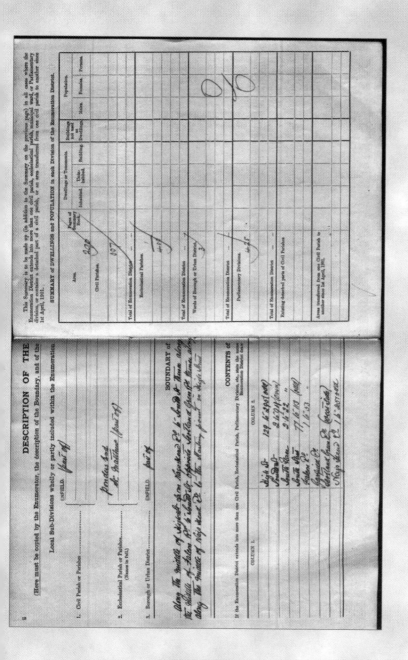

Figure 6-16 District dwellings

This is the sheet on the right hand side of the pair and this enumerator seems to have got away without filling in any of the information.

65

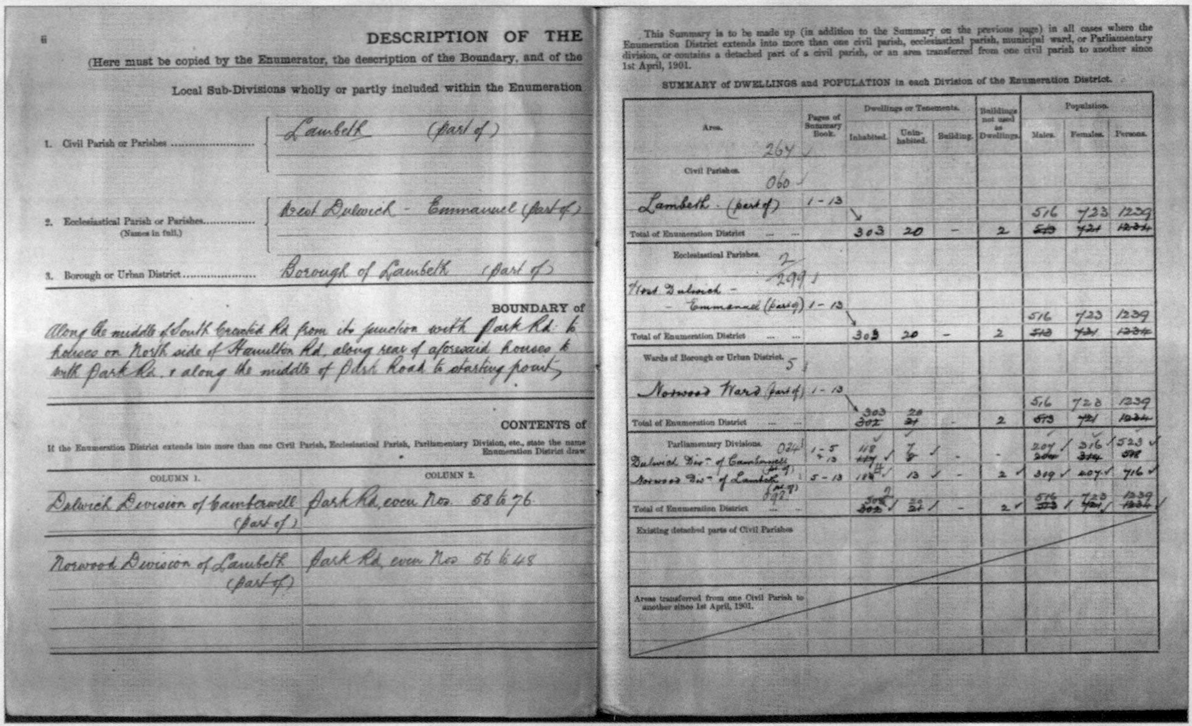

6

DESCRIPTION OF THE

(Here must be copied by the Enumerator, the description of the Boundary, and of the

Local Sub-Divisions wholly or partly included within the Enumeration

1. Civil Parish or Parishes .... Lambeth (part of)

2. Ecclesiastical Parish or Parishes .... (Names in full.) West Dulwich - Emmanuel (part of)

3. Borough or Urban District .... Borough of Lambeth (part of)

BOUNDARY of

Along the middle of South Croxted Rd from its junction with Park Rd. to houses on North side of Hamilton Rd. along rear of aforesaid houses to with Park Rd. & along the middle of Park Road to starting point.

CONTENTS of

If the Enumeration District extends into more than one Civil Parish, Ecclesiastical Parish, Parliamentary Division, etc., state the name Enumeration District draw

COLUMN 1.	COLUMN 2.
Dulwich Division of Camberwell (part of)	Park Rd, even Nos 58 to 76
Norwood Division of Lambeth (part of)	Park Rd, even Nos 56 to 48

This Summary is to be made up (in addition to the Summary on the previous page) in all cases where the Enumeration District extends into more than one civil parish, ecclesiastical parish, municipal ward, or Parliamentary division, or contains a detached part of a civil parish, or an area transferred from one civil parish to another since 1st April, 1901.

SUMMARY of DWELLINGS and POPULATION in each Division of the Enumeration District.

Area.	Pages of Summary Book.	Dwellings or Tenements. Inhabited.	Uninhabited.	Building.	Buildings not used as Dwellings.	Population. Males.	Females.	Persons.
264								
Civil Parishes. 060								
Lambeth (part of)	1 - 13					516	723	1239
Total of Enumeration District		303	20	-	2	513	721	1234
Ecclesiastical Parishes. 2								
2991 West Dulwich - Emmanuel (part of)	1 - 13					516	723	1239
Total of Enumeration District		303	20	-	2	513	721	1234
Wards of Borough or Urban District. 5								
Norwood Ward (part of)	1 - 13					516	723	1239
Total of Enumeration District		303 / 302	20 / 21	-	2	513	721	1234
Parliamentary Divisions. 024 Dulwich Div. of Camberwell (part of)	1 - 5 + 13	118 / 117	7 / 8	-	-	207 / 206	316 / 314	523 / 520
042 Norwood Div. of Lambeth (part of)	5 - 13	184	13	-	2	309	407	716
Total of Enumeration District		303 / 302	20 / 21	-	2	516 / 513	723 / 721	1239 / 1234
Existing detached parts of Civil Parishes								
Areas transferred from one Civil Parish to another since 1st April, 1901.								

Figure 6-17 District dwellings showing completed details

The one above shows a dwellings sheet where the information has been completed. The heading says that the information was to be completed where “the Enumeration District extends into more than one civil parish, ecclesiastical parish, municipal ward or Parliamentary division, or contains a detached part of a civil parish, or an area transferred from one civil parish to another since 1 April, 1901.”

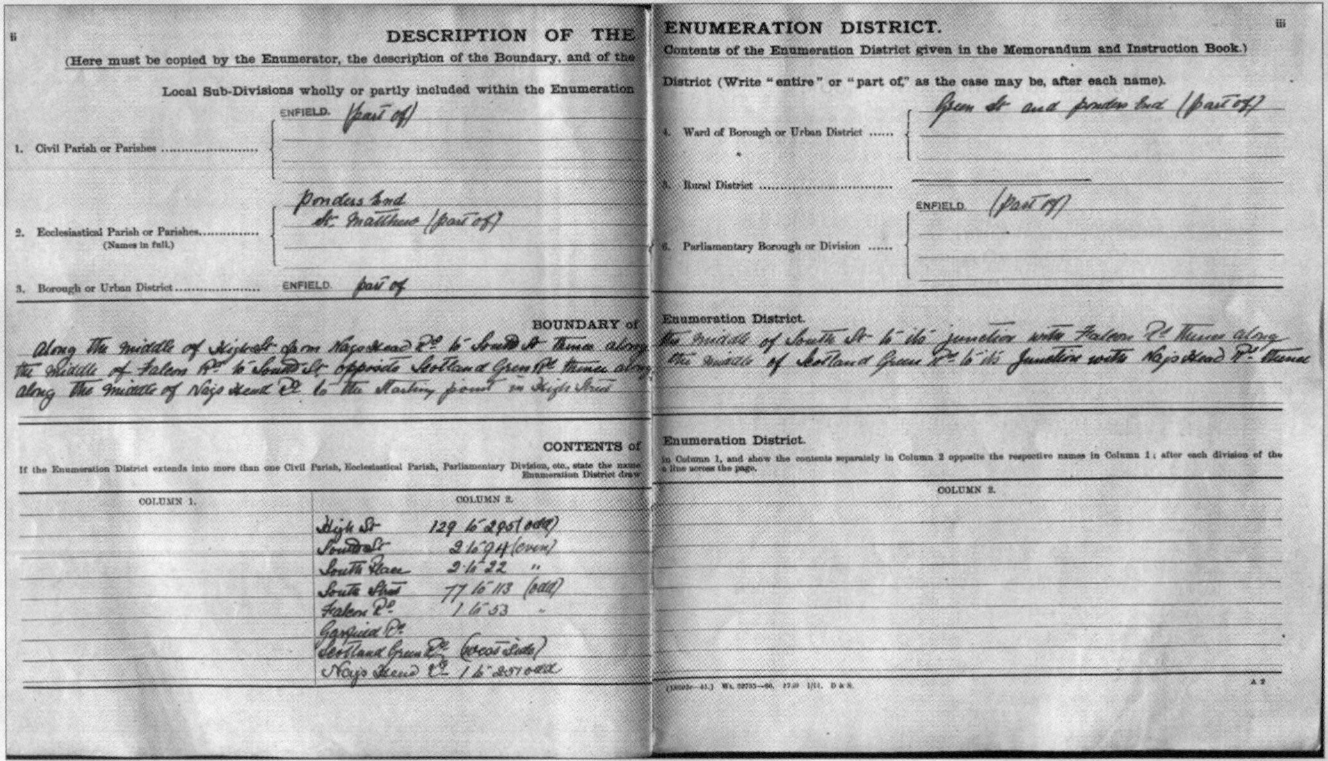
ii

DESCRIPTION OF THE ENUMERATION DISTRICT.

(Here must be copied by the Enumerator, the description of the Boundary, and of the Contents of the Enumeration District given in the Memorandum and Instruction Book.)

Local Sub-Divisions wholly or partly included within the Enumeration District (Write "entire" or "part of," as the case may be, after each name).

1. Civil Parish or Parishes .... ENFIELD. (part of)
2. Ecclesiastical Parish or Parishes .... (Names in full.) Ponders End St. Matthew (part of)
3. Borough or Urban District .... ENFIELD. part of
4. Ward of Borough or Urban District ...... Green St and Ponders End (part of)
5. Rural District ....
6. Parliamentary Borough or Division ...... ENFIELD. (part of)

BOUNDARY of Enumeration District.

Along the middle of High St from Nags Head Rd to South St thence along the middle of South St to its junction with Falcon Rd thence along the middle of Falcon Rd to South St opposite Scotland Green Rd thence along the middle of Scotland Green Rd to its junction with Nags Head Rd thence along the middle of Nags Head Rd to the starting point in High Street

CONTENTS of Enumeration District.

If the Enumeration District extends into more than one Civil Parish, Ecclesiastical Parish, Parliamentary Division, etc., state the name in Column 1, and show the contents separately in Column 2 opposite the respective names in Column 1; after each division of the Enumeration District draw a line across the page.

COLUMN 1.	COLUMN 2.	COLUMN 2.
	High St 129 to 295 (odd)	
	South St 2 to 94 (even)	
	South Place 2 to 22 "	
	South Street 77 to 113 (odd)	
	Falcon Rd 1 to 53 "	
	Garfield Rd	
	Scotland Green Rd (west side)	
	Nags Head Rd 1 to 25 odd	

(18002—41.) Wt. 32752—86. 17.0 1/11. D & S. A 2

iii

Figure 6-18 The district description

In the earlier censuses this was described as the 'enumerators walk' and explained the route that he walked around his area.

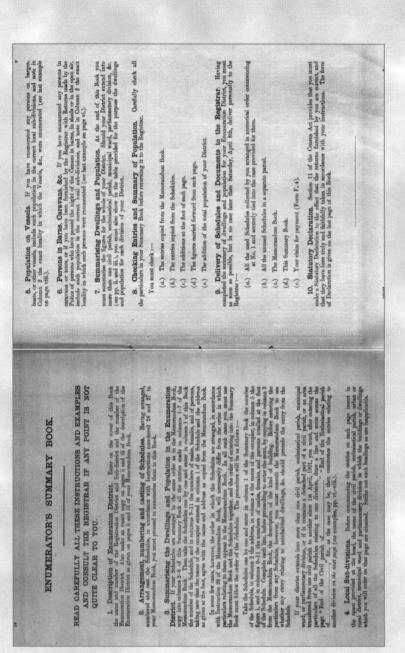

Figure 6-19 The enumerator's instructions

If you are very lucky then you might end up with the second part of the pages for District dwellings or District totals containing the printed instructions to the enumerator. Whether you will get both sides is doubtful. This has been made up from two halves found in different piece numbers.

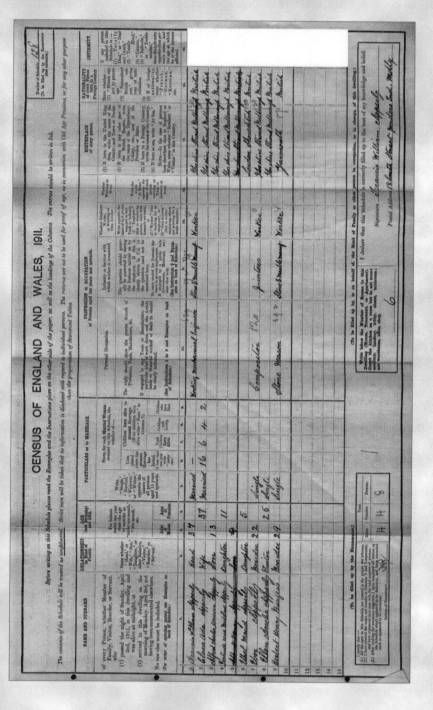

Figure 6-20 A household schedule
(See overleaf for descriptions)

69

Because we have the original schedules we will go through the layout as it is slightly different from that in previous years. You may just be able to make out the crease marks down the page. They run through columns 3, 10 and 13 and were folded to produce the cover shown in Figure 6-10

The first column was for the "… names of every person who spent the night of Sunday 2 April, 1911 or who arrived on Monday 3 April not having been enumerated elsewhere." There were examples on the back of the schedule (a copy of the back of the schedule is included as Figure 6-28 at the end of this chapter) as to how it should have been completed.

Of interest here is Albert Henry Apperly (line 5 of figure 6-20). The details have been completed in full and then crossed out so I can only assume that the form was completed before Albert went off to stay with his uncle, where I later found him. I have also seen schedules where the names of dead children have been included. A real boon if you weren't aware of them.

Column 2 has relationship to the head of the household. The list given on this form is quite short but unfortunately there are no relationship guidelines on the back of the form to help the householder. As I mentioned in Chapter 3, the list I have seen was quite extensive with many obscure relationships. Columns three and four have the age last birthday and of males and females in two separate columns. A person's sex was therefore assumed from the column their age was in. Whilst sex appears in the transcriptions it isn't a searchable option with this census. Column five has the marital status for all people over the age of fifteen.

Columns six to nine are the ones that are new in the 1911 census and these columns were only to be completed for married women. Therefore divorced or widowed women were not supposed to complete these fields, but many did. In some instances the data has also been entered against the husband in the family. In most of these cases the details have been crossed out by the enumerator when he checked the schedule but they are usually still readable.

Column six asks for the number of "completed years the present marriage has lasted". The question here is: Did they tell the truth? – and certainly if you can't find the marriage in the year implied in this column I would extend the search for it to other years. I have certainly found entries where the information is a complete lie. One couple said they had been married for ten years yet the marriage certificate I have for them showed that they were married in 1907! Mind you they did have three children born between 1901 and 1907 and were obviously trying to hide the fact that they married after these births. The last three columns of the set ask firstly for details of the "number of children born alive". In this case they have had six children and according to the next columns, four are still alive and two have died. At least the maths adds up! This actually bears out a story that my Grandfather used to tell of there being two more children who had died young. Now they weren't with the family in the 1901 census so were either born between their marriage in 1894 and 1901 or between 1901 and 1911. I am still trying to find out who they were.

Columns ten to thirteen cover the person's "profession or occupation". The first of these relates to the personal occupation and was to include the '"...precise branch..." and the "...kind of work done...". Examples and instructions were again included on the back of the schedule. The next column should "generally only be answered by stating the business carried on by the employer. If this is clearly shown in column 10 the question need not be answered." For children in education it is normally shown as 'School' rather than the word 'Scholar' which was used in previous censuses. I am not sure whether it was just left off this particular example or whether the children in this family didn't go to school.

In this example you will notice that Francis Apperly, the head of the household, is shown as being a 'Working Mechanical Engineer' employed in 'Stone & Marble Manufacture'. You might also be able to make out the numbers that were mentioned in Chapter 2, which were used to classify each occupation for statistical analysis. On the actual images these are shown in green and you maybe able to make them out on the front cover.

Column twelve asked whether the person was "employer, worker or working on own account", a question that first appeared in the 1901 census. Here all of the people in employment were shown as being workers. The last of the four columns should have the words 'at home' if the work was carried out there.

Column thirteen asked for the place of birth of every person. The instructions on the form say "if born in the United Kingdom – enter county and town or parish of birth", "if born in the British Empire – enter the name of the Dependency, Colony, etc and the Province or State", "if at sea – enter "at sea"" and finally "if in a Foreign Country – enter the name of the country".

This obviously led to some confusion, even with Francis, as he gives his place of birth as 'Glos shire Stroud Rodborough'. The first is, of course, one of the common variants for the county of Gloucestershire and certainly if you look for him being born simply in Gloucestershire then it will still find him. The common variations for all counties are recognised. The place name though is a little more confusing as Rodborough is part of Stroud and possibly should have been left as Rodborough.

I have seen the place of birth entered as simply 'London' but I have also seen it as the actual street! Some birth places are still as mis-leading as they have been in the earlier censuses. What is new is the addition of the codes. These are shown in red on the images, and as stated earlier, they can be used in the search screens. Do be aware though that some of the entries do not appear to have codes.

The next field, column fifteen, was for Nationality and was only to be completed "… for people born in a foreign country". What should appear is "British subject by parentage", "Naturalised British – including the year of naturalisation" or "French, German, etc". Francis here was obviously confused by the question or maybe just wanted to make a point. This is the sort of question that crops up all too often when reading returns and which we will never know the answers to.

The last column is the one that we will have to wait till 2012 for as it is the one that the Information Commissioner's Office said was to be withheld. It contains the details as to whether the person was deaf, dumb, lunatic, imbecile, etc. What is interesting from my point of view is that in many cases we as family historians probably already know that information. The information isn't always hidden though, as I have seen institutions where 'Lunatic' is listed as the occupation. I can only assume, at this point in time, that the information has been transcribed already and that it will be included in the transcriptions after 2012.

Across the bottom of the schedule there are two boxes. The first was completed by the enumerator and shows the total number of males, females and a grand total. Enumerators all had to initial the return to show that

1 "… all the ages were entered in the correct columns"
2 "… the number of males and females agreed"
3 "after making enquiries … they had corrected any entries on the schedule that appeared to be defective…"

The box on the right has the details of the number of rooms in the property. It was to include the kitchen but not the scullery, landing, lobby, closet, bathroom nor workshops, offices, etc. To the right is the signature of the head of the household and below that the address that the return relates to. It appears from some of the transcriptions that this space was a little on the small side at times and did lead to some of the addresses being truncated.

The household schedule, shown here, was the major one used but not the only one by any means as was described in Chapter 1. We will now have a look at some of the more common of the other forms used and explain the differences.

Large premises schedules (Shown in figure 6-21)

There is really only one major difference in the schedules that go over more than one page and that is that the address, the signature of the head of the household and the statistical information all appear on the last page. Now for a 40 person schedule that isn't too bad as it is only one extra image. If you just want the name of the property then it will appear in the transcription of page one.

The problem though, and I can only comment on the situation at the time of writing, occurs when it comes to the larger schedule still which catered for a household of up to 100 people. If your person is on the first page and you want the signature of the person completing the schedule as well, you have to also purchase all of the intervening pages. The same applies if your person is on one of the later pages and you want to see the details of the head of the household on page one. Hopefully that will change.

Institutions (shown in figure 6-22)

All the information columns are exactly the same as the standard schedule. The same comments apply as for the larger premises schedules explained above.

Military schedule (shown in figures 6-23 and 6-24)

This first of these is for Arthur William Halstead. Whilst he is at the Delhi Barracks, South Tedworth, Hampshire he isn't actually in the army and the schedule is very similar to the normal household one but for a military establishment. Arthur is a Grocer by profession.

The second is for Robert Edward Halstead who was a Lance Corporal in the 7th Queens Own Hussars and based at Hounslow. As this return is for army personnel the return is different in that a lot of the columns in the other returns are not required. The columns in this type of schedule are Name, Rank, Age last birthday, Marital condition, Unit or arm of service, Trade and Birthplace.

Like the large households and institutions that are multipage there is no easy way of getting to the first or last page without going through the entire set of intervening images.

Shipping schedule (shown in Figures 6-25 and 6-26)

Again I have included two examples. In both cases they are listed in the indexes as a schedule type 'Shipping'.

The first is for John Halstead on a canal boat on 'The Canal, Calder, Yorkshire'. The second is for William Halstead Merannis based in Southampton, Hampshire. In both cases the schedules are identical to the normal in terms of the columns. The exception is that it clearly says in the box on the top left that it is a 'shipping schedule for up to 100 people'.

Welsh schedules (Figure 6-27)

Now I know that the Welsh counties aren't there yet and may be a while in coming but I do have a copy of one and it is worth showing and commenting on as it may well explain some of the problems that may occur with them. When it was announced that you could apply for a copy schedule under the Freedom of Information Act, Graham, the third member of the Census Detectives team, applied for the one for the house that his grandparents lived in, as the family were there for more than thirty years. Typically, it didn't answer the questions that he had and only threw up more! However, it did show that there is an additional column on the end which asks whether they spoke 'English, Welsh or both'. No entry was required here for children under the age of three.

This may explain why some of the Welsh counties may be taking longer than expected to transcribe as something like 50% of the schedules are in Welsh itself. FindMyPast are working with the Welsh family history societies to help ensure that the correct translations are made. The transcripts will still be 'as seen', in other words in Welsh, but the search engine will look for the English equivalent if that is what you entered.

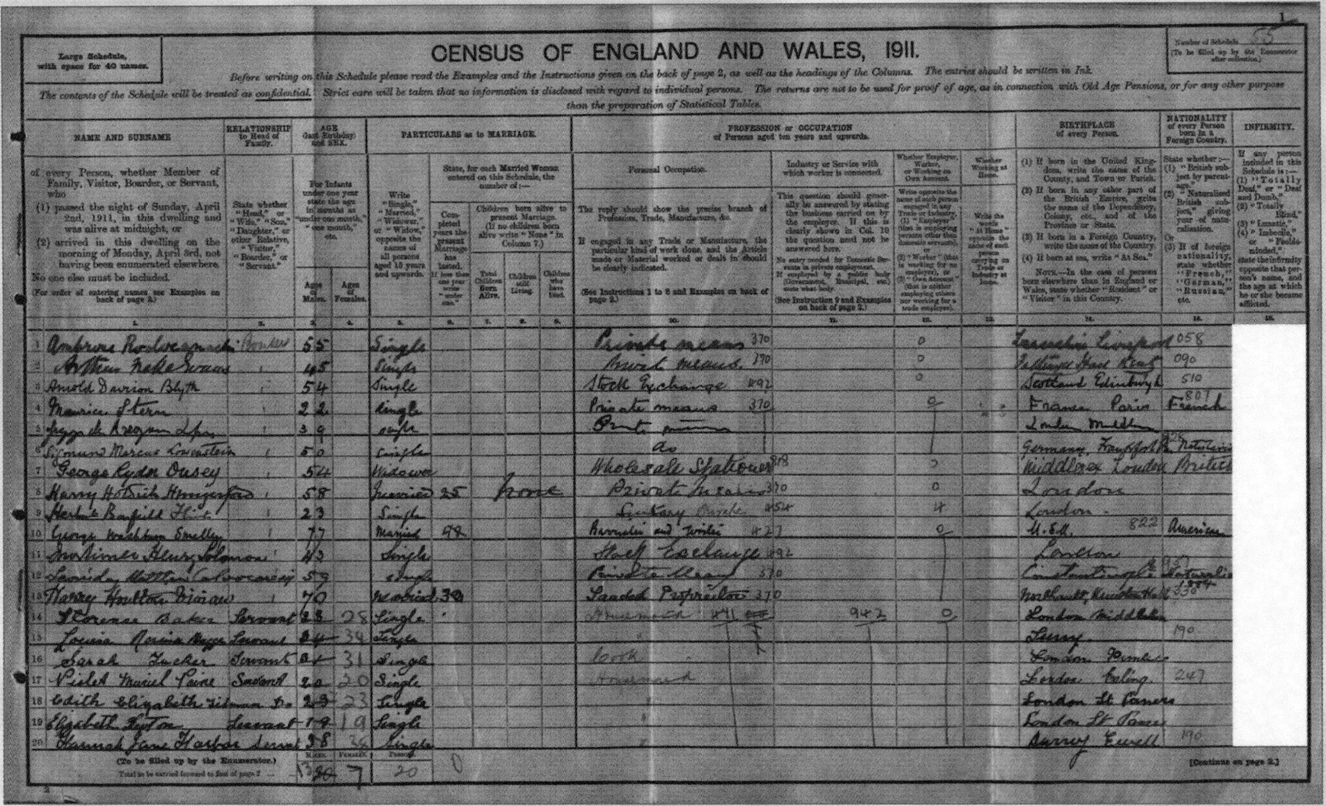
Large Schedule, with space for 40 names.

Number of Schedule 55 (To be filled up by the Enumerator after collection.)

CENSUS OF ENGLAND AND WALES, 1911.

Before writing on this Schedule please read the Examples and the Instructions given on the back of page 2, as well as the headings of the Columns. The entries should be written in Ink.

The contents of the Schedule will be treated as confidential. Strict care will be taken that no information is disclosed with regard to individual persons. The returns are not to be used for proof of age, as in connection with Old Age Pensions, or for any other purpose than the preparation of Statistical Tables.

	Name and Surname	Relationship to Head of Family	Age (Males)	Age (Females)	Marriage	Years married	Children	Personal Occupation	Industry	Employer/Worker	At Home	Birthplace	Nationality
1	Ambrose Rosliwegauch	Boarder	55		Single			Private means 370		0		Lancashire Liverpool 058	
2	Arthur Neale Simms		45		Single			Private means 370		0		Fellingen Hesse Kent 090	
3	Arnold Davison Blyth		54		Single			Stock Exchange 892		0		Scotland Edinburgh 510	
4	Maurice Stern		22		Single			Private means 370		0		France Paris 801	French
5	[illegible]		39		Single			[illegible]				London Middlesex	
6	Sigmund Marcus Lowenstein		50		Single			do				Germany Frankfort 802	Naturalised
7	George Lyon Dusey		54		Widower			Wholesale Stationer 808		0		Middlesex London	British
8	Harry Hetrich Hungerford		58		Married	25	None	Private means 370		0		London	
9	Herbert Banfield Flint		23		Single			[illegible] 854		W		London	
10	George Washburn Smalley		77		Married	48		Journalist and writer 427		0		U.S.A. 822	American
11	Justinian Henry Solomon		43		Single			Stock Exchange 892				London	
12	Leonidas Mitton Calvocoressi		59		Single			Private means 370				Constantinople 837	Naturalised 1884
13	Harry Hamilton Bisiaw		70		Married	30		Landed Proprietor 370				Northcourt, Huntsham 330	
14	Florence Baker	Servant	28	28	Single			Housemaid 841	942	0		London Middlesex	
15	Louisa Rosina Maggs	Servant	34	34	Single							Surrey 190	
16	Sarah Tucker	Servant	31	31	Single			Cook				London Pimlico	
17	Violet Muriel Paine	Servant	20	20	Single			Housemaid				London Ealing 247	
18	Edith Elizabeth Tidman	Do	23	23	Single							London St Pancras	
19	Elizabeth Lyton	Servant	19	19	Single							London St Pancras	
20	Hannah Jane Harbor	Servant	38	36	Single							Surrey Ewell 190	

(To be filled up by the Enumerator.) Total to be carried forward to foot of page 3 — Males 13 7, Females 7, Persons 20

[Continue on page 2.]

Figure 6-21 A schedule for a household of up to 40 persons

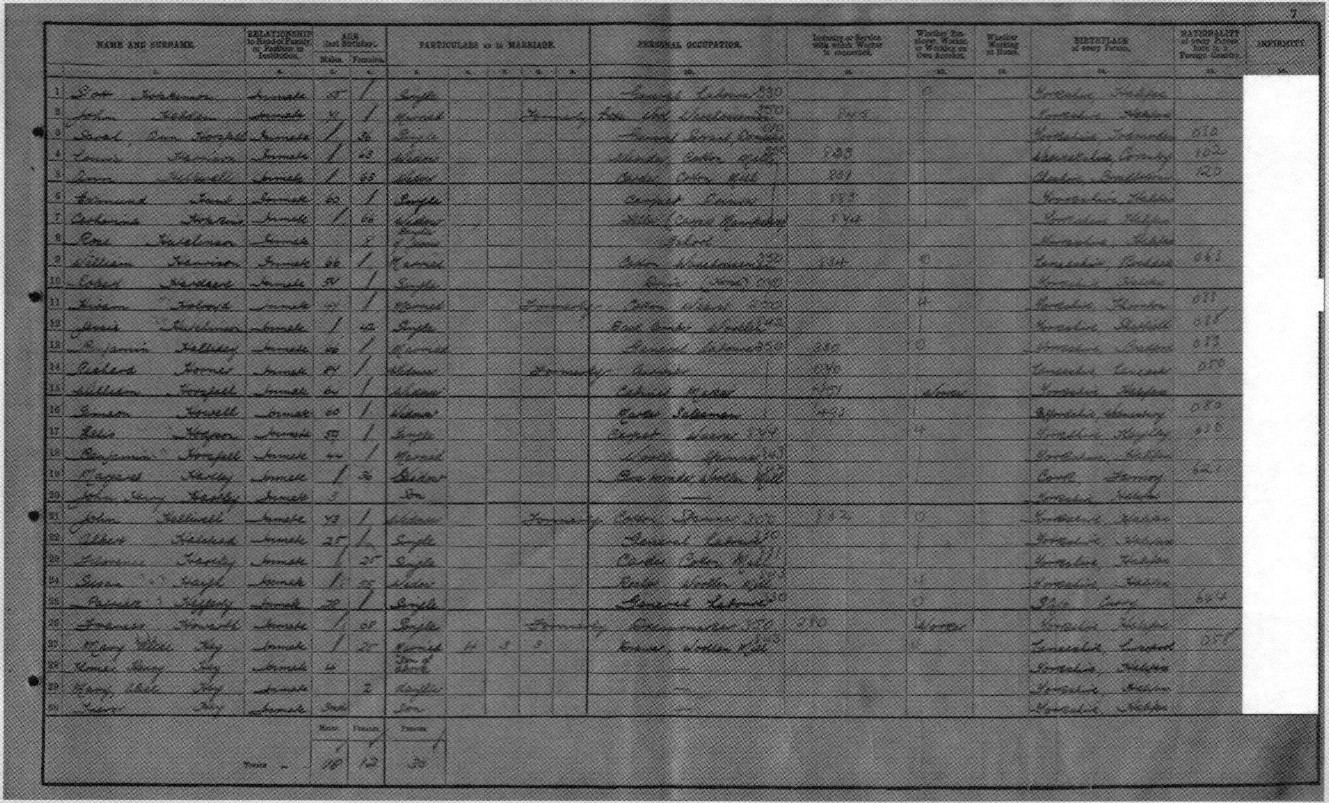

Figure 6-22 *An institution schedule*

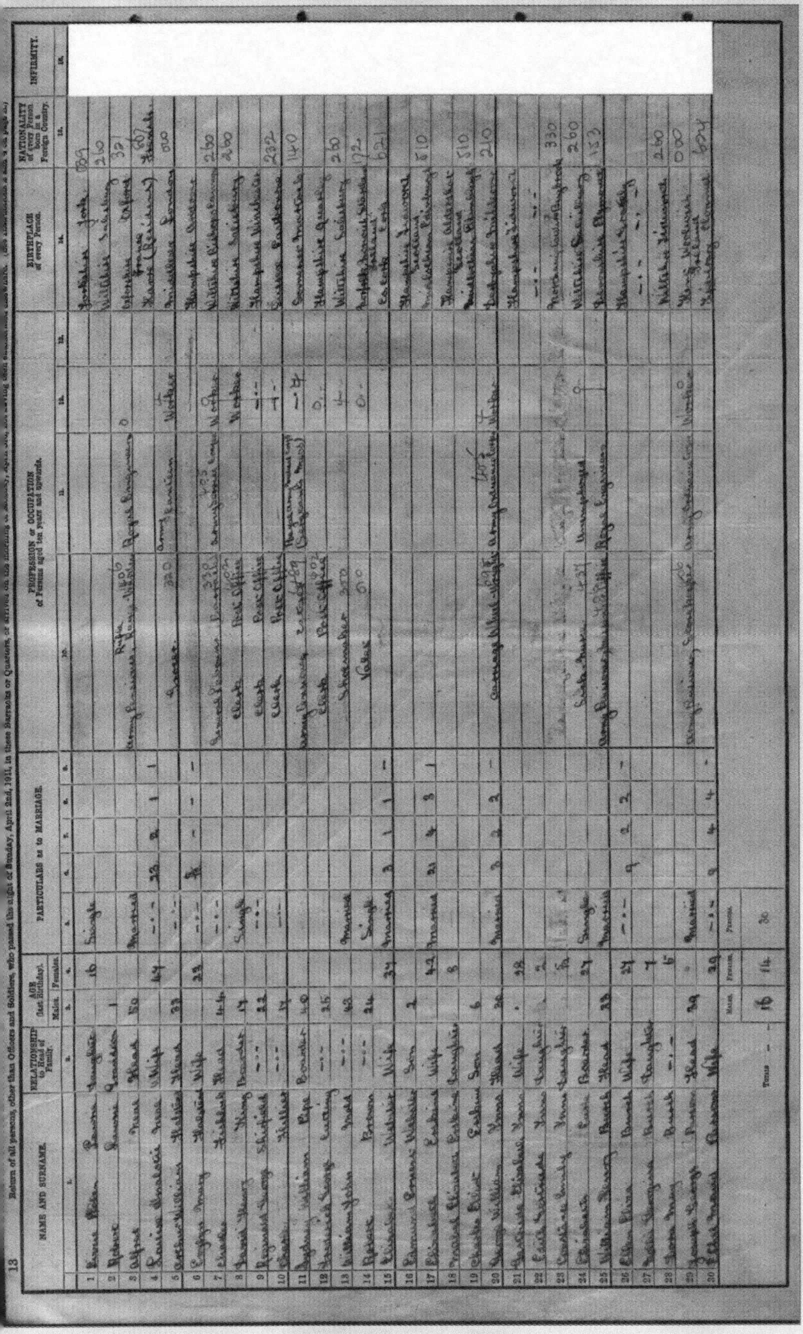

Figure 6-23 A military schedule showing non-military personnel

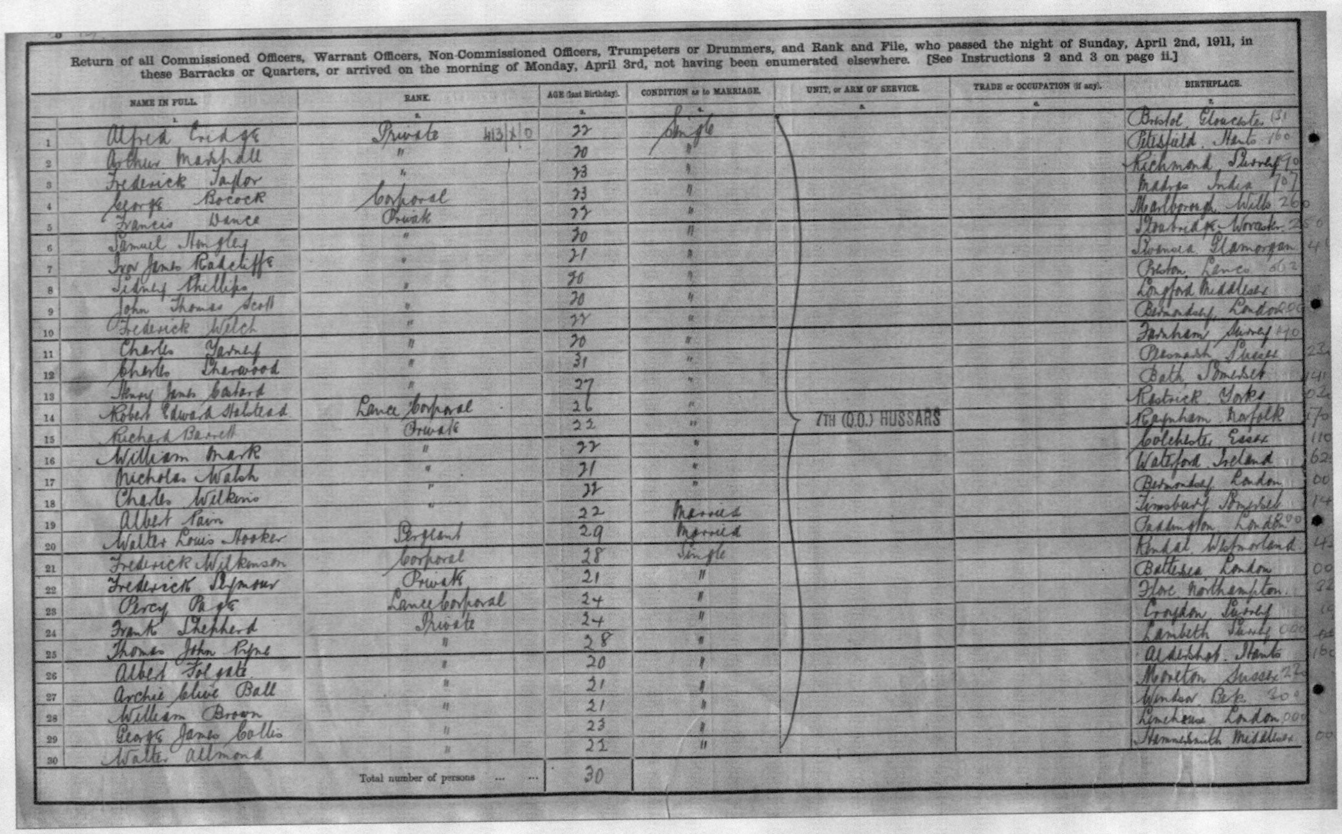

Return of all Commissioned Officers, Warrant Officers, Non-Commissioned Officers, Trumpeters or Drummers, and Rank and File, who passed the night of Sunday, April 2nd, 1911, in these Barracks or Quarters, or arrived on the morning of Monday, April 3rd, not having been enumerated elsewhere. [See Instructions 2 and 3 on page ii.]

	NAME IN FULL. 1.	RANK. 2.	AGE (last Birthday). 3.	CONDITION as to MARRIAGE. 4.	UNIT, or ARM OF SERVICE. 5.	TRADE or OCCUPATION (if any). 6.	BIRTHPLACE. 7.
1	Alfred Cridge	Private 413	22	Single	7TH (Q.O.) HUSSARS		Bristol Gloucester
2	Arthur Marshall	"	20	"			Petersfield Hants
3	Frederick Taylor	"	23	"			Richmond Surrey
4	George Bocock	Corporal	23	"			Madras India
5	Francis Dance	Private	22	"			Marlborough Wilts
6	Samuel Hingley	"	20	"			Stourbridge Worcester
7	Ivor James Radcliffe	"	21	"			Swansea Glamorgan
8	Sidney Phillips	"	20	"			Preston Lancs
9	John Thomas Scott	"	20	"			Longford Middlesex
10	Frederick Welch	"	22	"			Bermondsey London
11	Charles Yarney	"	20	"			Farnham Surrey
12	Charles Sherwood	"	31	"			Bosham Sussex
13	Henry James Catford	"	27	"			Bath Somerset
14	Robert Edward Halstead	Lance Corporal	26	"			Rastrick Yorks
15	Richard Barrett	Private	22	"			Raynham Norfolk
16	William Mark	"	22	"			Colchester Essex
17	Nicholas Walsh	"	21	"			Waterford Ireland
18	Charles Wilkins	"	22	"			Bermondsey London
19	Albert Pain	"	22	Married			Tisbury Bristol
20	Walter Louis Hooker	Sergeant	29	Married			Paddington London
21	Frederick Wilkinson	Corporal	28	Single			Kendal Westmorland
22	Frederick Seymour	Private	21	"			Battersea London
23	Percy Page	Lance Corporal	24	"			Flore Northampton
24	Frank Shepherd	Private	24	"			Croydon Surrey
25	Thomas John Pyne	"	28	"			Lambeth Surrey
26	Albert Folgate	"	20	"			Aldershot Hants
27	Archie Clive Ball	"	21	"			Moreton Sussex
28	William Brown	"	21	"			Windsor Berks
29	George James Collis	"	23	"			Limehouse London
30	Walter Allmond	"	22	"			Hammersmith Middlesex
	Total number of persons		30				

Figure 6-24 A military schedule showing serving personnel

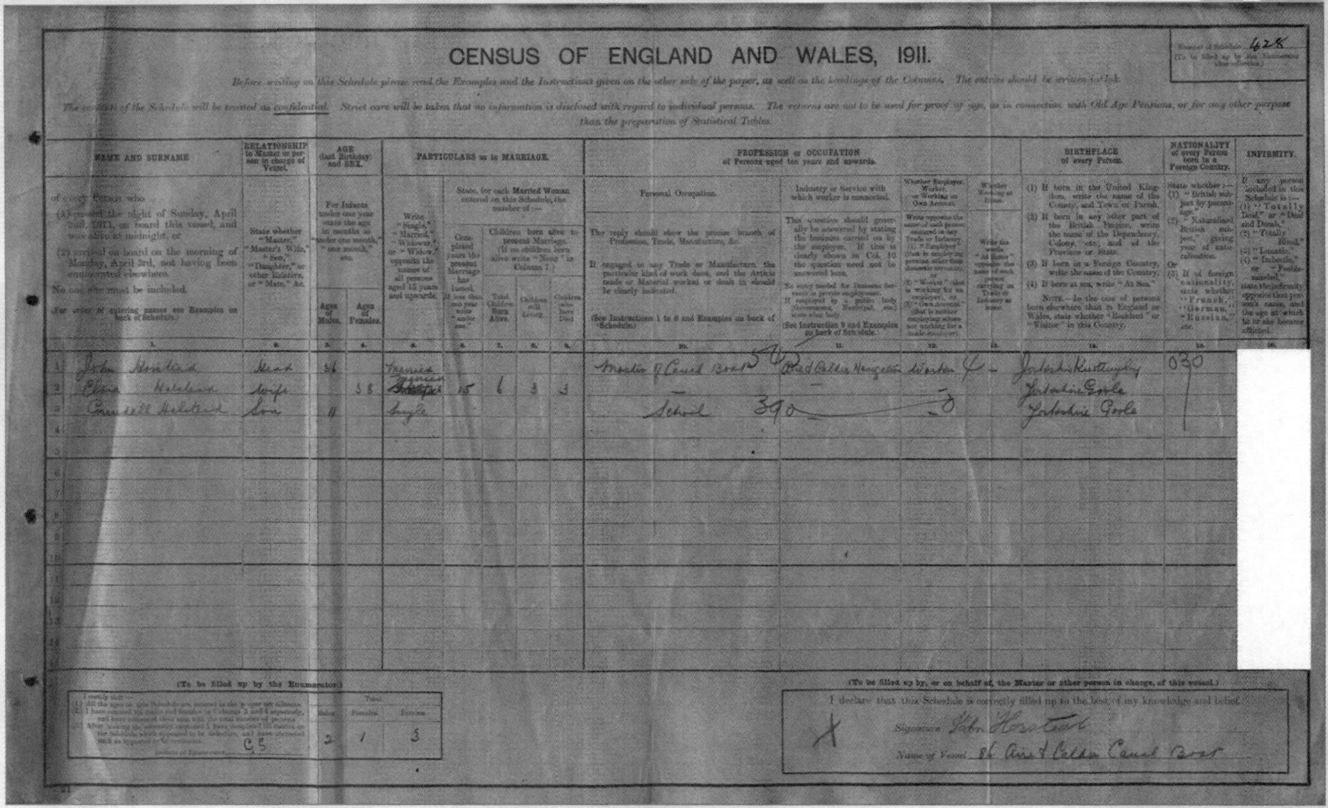
CENSUS OF ENGLAND AND WALES, 1911.

Before writing on this Schedule please read the Examples and the Instructions given on the other side of the paper, as well as the headings of the Columns. The entries should be written in Ink.

The contents of the Schedule will be treated as confidential. Strict care will be taken that no information is disclosed with regard to individual persons. The returns are not to be used for proof of age, as in connection with Old Age Pensions, or for any other purpose than the preparation of Statistical Tables.

Number of Schedule 428

NAME AND SURNAME	RELATIONSHIP to Master or person in charge of Vessel	AGE (last Birthday) and SEX: Ages of Males	Ages of Females	PARTICULARS as to MARRIAGE	Completed years the present Marriage has lasted	Total Children Born Alive	Children still Living	Children who have Died	Personal Occupation	Industry or Service with which worker is connected	Whether Employer, Worker, or Working on Own Account	Whether Working at Home	BIRTHPLACE of every Person	NATIONALITY of every Person born in a Foreign Country	INFIRMITY
John Horstead	Head	36		Married					Master of Canal Boat	Aire & Calder Navigation	Worker		Yorkshire Knottingley	030	
Eliza Horstead	Wife		38	Married	15	6	3	3					Yorkshire Goole		
Crandell Horstead	Son	11		Single					School				Yorkshire Goole		

(To be filled up by the Enumerator.) Total: Males 2, Females 1, Persons 3. C.S.

(To be filled up by, or on behalf of, the Master or other person in charge of this vessel.)

I declare that this Schedule is correctly filled up to the best of my knowledge and belief.

Signature John Horstead

Name of Vessel 86 Aire & Calder Canal Boat

Figure 6-25 A shipping schedule for a canal boat

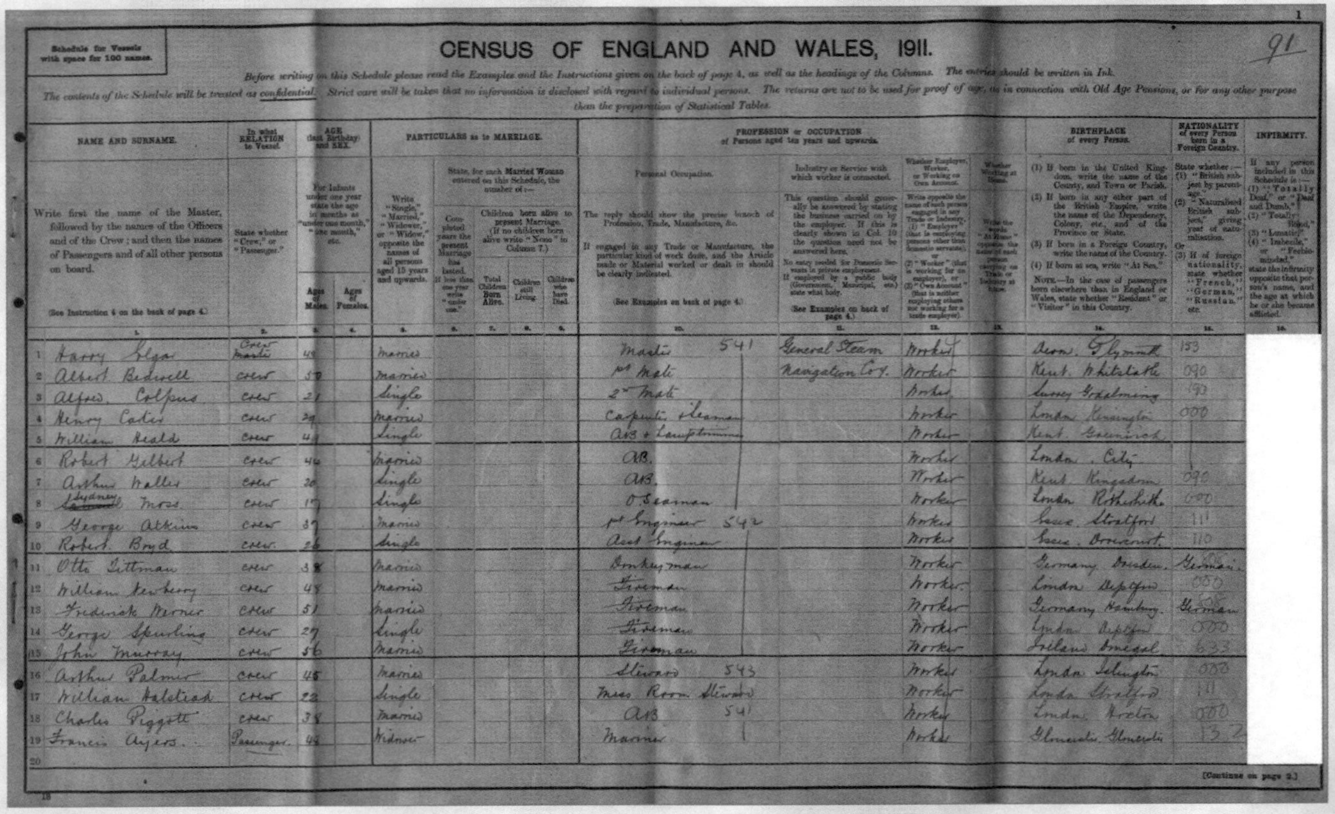

Schedule for Vessels with space for 100 names.

CENSUS OF ENGLAND AND WALES, 1911.

91

Before writing on this Schedule please read the Examples and the Instructions given on the back of page 4, as well as the headings of the Columns. The entries should be written in Ink.

The contents of the Schedule will be treated as confidential. Strict care will be taken that no information is disclosed with regard to individual persons. The returns are not to be used for proof of age, as in connection with Old Age Pensions, or for any other purpose than the preparation of Statistical Tables.

	NAME AND SURNAME.	In what RELATION to Vessel.	AGE (last Birthday) and SEX. Ages of Males.	Ages of Females.	PARTICULARS as to MARRIAGE.	Completed years the present Marriage has lasted.	Total Children Born Alive.	Children still Living.	Children who have Died.	PROFESSION or OCCUPATION: Personal Occupation.	Industry or Service with which worker is connected.	Whether Employer, Worker, or Working on Own Account.	Whether Working at Home.	BIRTHPLACE of every Person.	NATIONALITY of every Person born in a Foreign Country.	INFIRMITY.
	1.	2.	3.	4.	5.	6.	7.	8.	9.	10.	11.	12.	13.	14.	15.	16.
1	Harry Elgar	Crew Master	49		Married					Master 541	General Steam	Worker		Devon Plymouth	153	
2	Albert Bedwell	Crew	50		Married					1st Mate	Navigation Coy.	Worker		Kent Whitstable	090	
3	Alfred Colpus	Crew	21		Single					2nd Mate		Worker		Surrey Godalming	193	
4	Henry Cotis	Crew	29		Married					Carpenter Seaman		Worker		London Kensington	000	
5	William Heald	Crew	41		Single					AB + Lamptrimmer		Worker		Kent Greenwich		
6	Robert Gilbert	Crew	46		Married					AB.		Worker		London City		
7	Arthur Waller	Crew	20		Single					AB.		Worker		Kent Kingsdown	090	
8	Sydney Moss	Crew	17		Single					O Seaman		Worker		London Rotherhithe	000	
9	George Atkins	Crew	37		Married					1st Engineer 542		Worker		Essex Stratford	111	
10	Robert Boyd	Crew	26		Single					Asst Engineer		Worker		Essex Broomhill	110	
11	Otto Gittman	Crew	38		Married					Donkeyman		Worker		Germany Dresden	German	
12	William Newberry	Crew	48		Married					Fireman		Worker		London Deptford	000	
13	Frederick Werner	Crew	51		Married					Fireman		Worker		Germany Hamburg	German	
14	George Spurling	Crew	27		Single					Fireman		Worker		London Deptford	000	
15	John Murray	Crew	56		Married					Fireman		Worker		Ireland Donegal	633	
16	Arthur Palmer	Crew	45		Married					Steward 543		Worker		London Islington	000	
17	William Halstead	Crew	22		Single					Mess Room Steward		Worker		London Stratford	111	
18	Charles Piggott	Crew	38		Married					AB 541		Worker		London Hoxton	000	
19	Francis Ayers	Passenger	48		Widower					Mariner		Worker		Gloucester Gloucester	132	
20																

[Continue on page 2.]

Figure 6-26 A shipping schedule for a vessel

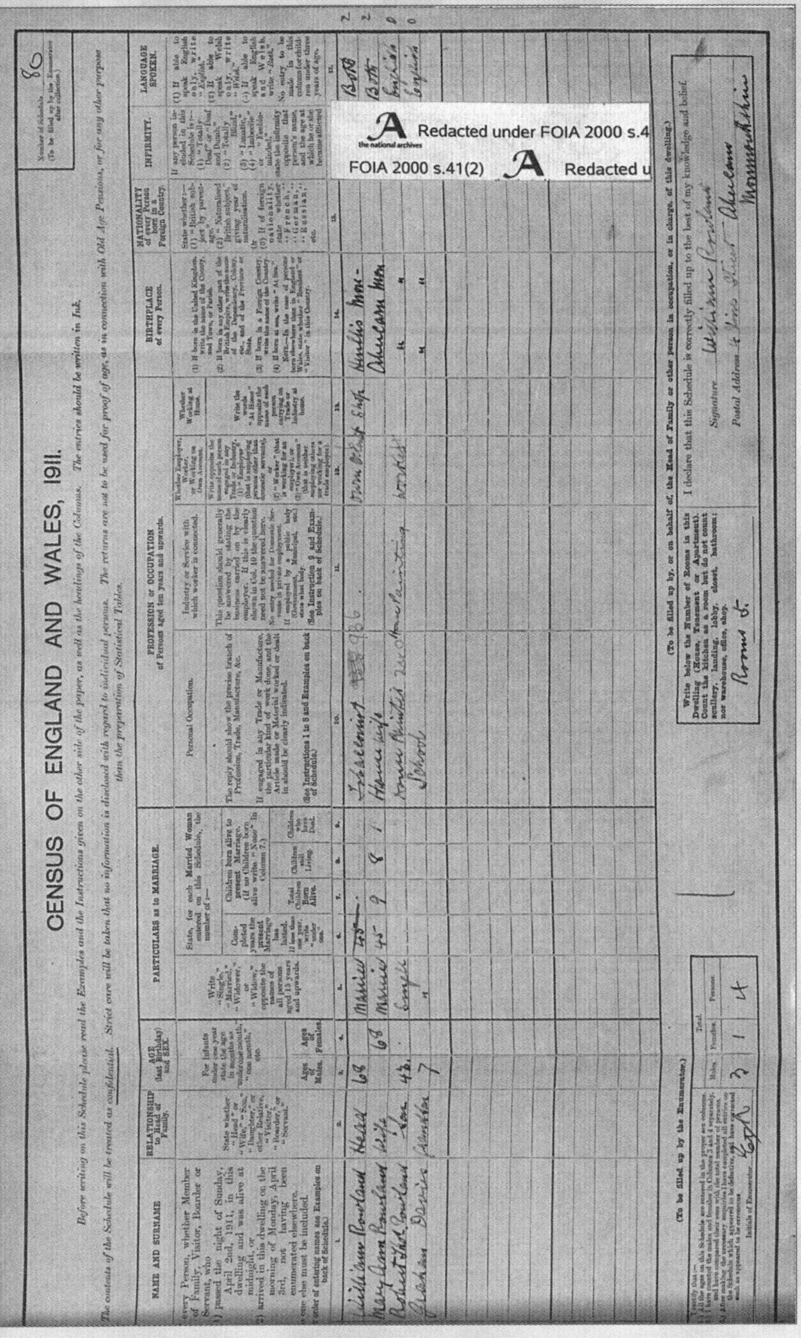

CENSUS OF ENGLAND AND WALES, 1911.

Before writing on this Schedule please read the Examples and the Instructions given on the other side of the paper, as well as the headings of the Columns. The entries should be written in Ink.

The contents of the Schedule will be treated as confidential. Strict care will be taken that no information is disclosed with regard to individual persons. The returns are not to be used for proof of age, or in connection with Old Age Pensions, or for any other purpose than the preparation of Statistical Tables.

Redacted under FOIA 2000 s.4

FOIA 2000 s.41(2) — Redacted u

Figure 6-27 A Welsh schedule

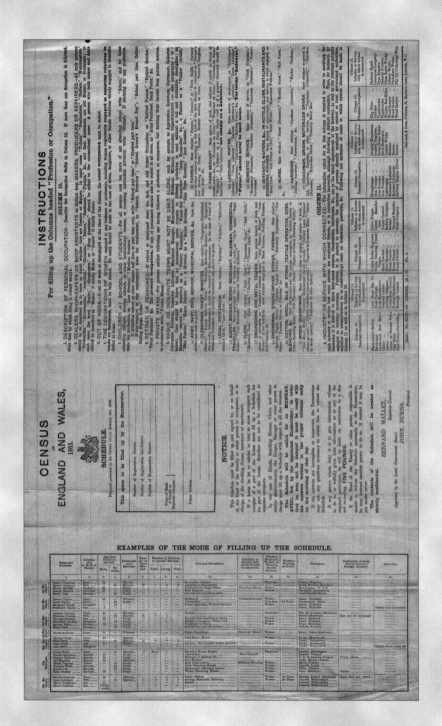

Figure 6-28 The back of the schedule showing the examples

The place in the second column is what has been taken out to make the cover image for the schedule

82

CHAPTER 7

My records

The one advantage of the 1911 site over FindMyPast is that it remembers what records you have viewed already. This is reminiscent of the ScotlandsPeople web site, also maintained by brightsolid (as you will remember from Chapter 1) the parent company behind both sites.

It is nice to be able to check whether you have looked at something already. If you do find an index entry where you have already looked at the transcription or image then the index view will show it as already having been paid for (see figure 3-3 in Chapter 3).

This is where the 'My records' tab comes in. Overleaf are two views of the screen. It is too long to show in one (containing 10 entries all the same format).

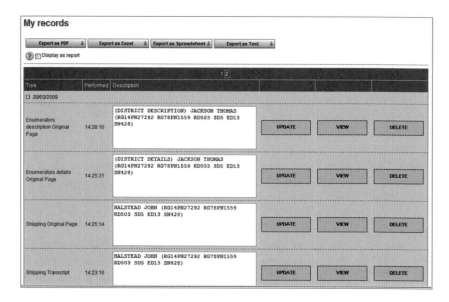

Figure 7-1 The top of the my records screen

The dark blue line at the top of the screen tells you how many pages of records there are (in this case two) and which page you are on. If you should get to more than 12 pages of entries then a small icon appears that lets you go to the next 12 pages and so on.

You will also notice that each date has a small icon, like a minus sign, to its left. By clicking on this the entries for that date will be hidden. They can be made to re-appear by clicking on the new icon which is like a 'plus' sign.

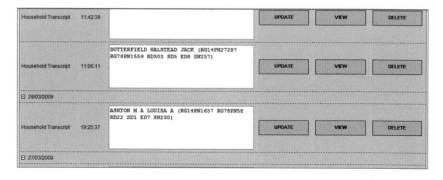

Figure 7-2 The bottom of the my records screen

The records have a divider showing the date on which the subsequent entries were generated. Each line is then made up in the same format.

♦ The type of image (whether it is a transcript, original page, enumeration district page and so on)
♦ The time that it was first viewed
♦ The name of the person that the entry related to
♦ An 'update' button
♦ A View button. This lets you view the entry again at no cost.
♦ A delete button. With this you can delete an entry that you may have looked at in error. One that maybe you thought was an ancestor yet turned out not to be and you don't want to clutter up the file with it again. However, do treat this with care and bear in mind that if you remove the entry from here you will be charged if you should want to look at it again.

You may have noticed this towards the top of the screen just above the dark blue bar. By clicking in the box on the left your screen will change to the one shown below which displays the same information, but in a report style format.

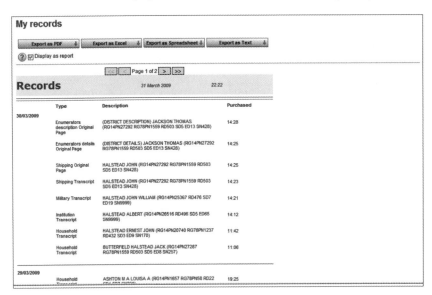

Figure 7-3 The my records screen as a report

The report format is much better to print from than the initial screen that was displayed. After all you don't really want the information on the right of each line in your printout.

You will also have noticed the line of icons above the report button. These give you the ability to view on screen or save the listing in the 'my records' screen to a file in a number of different formats. PDF will require you to have a PDF viewer installed on your machine. Excel will require an application to open an Excel formatted file. The spreadsheet option downloads the data as a CSV (comma separated variable) formatted file, which will normally also open in Excel. Lastly the text option will download the file as a tab separated text file.

In each case you will be presented with a screen similar to the one below for the PDF format.

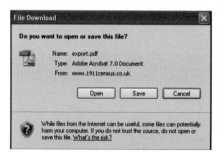

The Cancel button is obvious and will close the window and take you back to the 'my records' screen. The open button will download the information and open it in the required application and the save button will produce the normal Windows file save dialogue asking where you want the file to be saved.

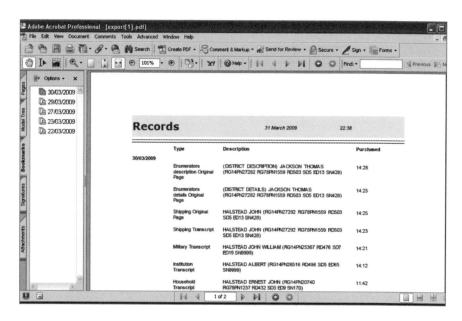

Figure 7-4 My records as a PDF report

The PDF formatted report has bookmarks for each date that you have viewed transcriptions or images. The details of all of the viewed material are included in the download. It tells you the type, description and time of the viewing for each event.

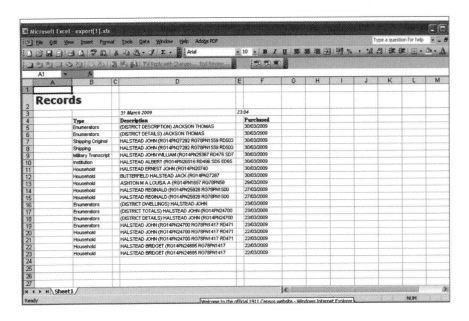

Figure 7-5 My records screen as an Excel downloaded file

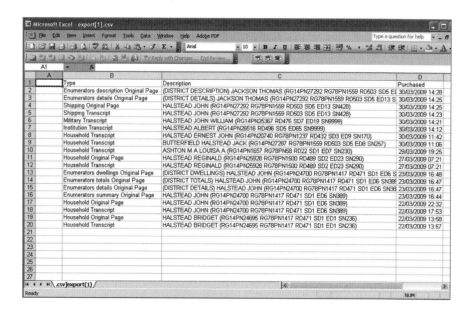

Figure 7-6 My records screen as a spreadsheet download

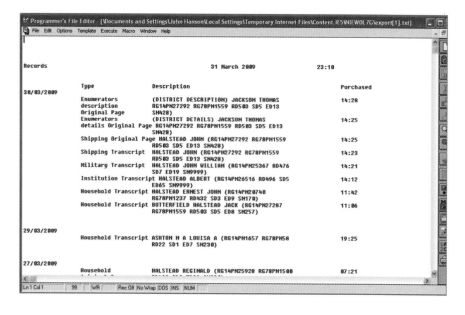

Figure 7-7 My records screen as a txt file

88

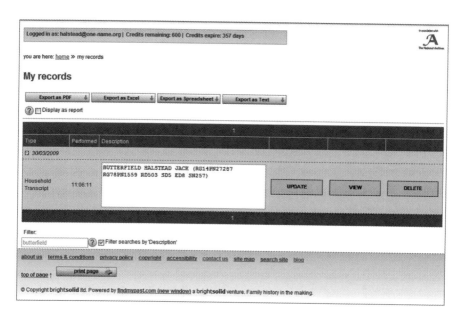

Figure 7-8 My records screen showing 'filtering'

CHAPTER 8
Why can't I find them?

I suspect that most of us find 80-85% of people who we are looking for first time. Although I suppose that if all of your ancestors were Smith, Brown and Jones then you might have a bigger problem.

Here I want to explore some of the reasons why you might not find an ancestor. Some may seem common sense but they do get forgotten. So bear with me if you think that I am stating the obvious. I will also add some tricks that the Census Detectives use to try and solve problems.

Has it been digitised yet?

As I said it might sound like stating the obvious, but is the county/area where you think they might be living actually online yet? Whilst some 90% of the country is now covered, there are still Wales, Channel Islands, Isle of Man, Royal Navy and military establishments overseas to come and in that order. The latest update in the blog at the beginning of April 2009 says that they hope to have the first parts of Wales online by the end of May.

It wasn't until the beginning of April, with the release of Northumberland, that I managed to track down a missing group in my wife's family. They were born, married and died in the Edmonton area of London, with the first child born there in 1908. Yet their second child was born in North Shields

in 1910 and the family were there in 1911. I could understand it if he had a job that required him to have moved all that way at that time but according to the 1911 census he was simply a Barman.

Are there any missing piece numbers?

Some of the census returns were water damaged before they were received by The National Archives. According to the 1911 census website "The collection of household schedules is complete, although around five per cent sustained water damage many years ago. All records have been scanned and transcribed, though inevitably the water-damaged documents are of poorer quality."

There are also a number of missing Enumerators' Summary Books (RG78). These are detailed on the 1911 census web site but are repeated here.

Buckinghamshire:	Amersham
Cambridgeshire:	Leverington, Walpole St Peter
Devonshire:	Okehampton
Cheshire:	Lymm, Budworth, Runcorn
Glamorganshire:	Central Cardiff
Leicestershire:	Lutterworth
Lincolnshire	(unspecified registration sub-districts)
Somersetshire:	Keynsham, Long Ashton
Staffordshire:	Repton, Tamworth
Warwickshire:	Atherstone
Yorkshire,	West Riding: Norton

This means that they will never be available online, and the original household return will be the only page that you will be able to get when paying for an image.

It also means that in a few cases you will not be able to find a household through the 'residential place' field by using certain names such as the civil parish as these were transcribed from the Enumerators' Summary Books.

Too much information

One of the biggest culprits causing failed searches is that people put too much information into the search screen. One has to remember that computers are dumb machines and can only do what the program tells them to do using the information provided. Also remember that when it comes to searching, it will want to match every letter that you have entered. Therefore the more you put in the greater the chance that you will not find what you want. There is a phrase that The Census Detectives use and that is 'Least is Best'.

From experience the Census Detectives have learnt that it is easier to add more information to reduce a list than it is to take information away from a fully completed search screen. Let me try and explain with the following example from my family. All of the examples below are simply looking for a name ignoring all other information.

If I take my maternal grandmothers family as an example we may be able to explain better. Her father's name was George Bird with 1293 entries. There are 157 Marias, which was her mother's name, but if I put in her full name of Maria Charlotte there isn't one. There is a Charlotte Maria but if I search for her with a George in the same household there are no matches so it is unlikely that she is the right one and mine will be simply listed as Maria. George and Maria and the three eldest children were all born in Suffolk but the youngest was born in Edmonton.

Of the children, all of whom lived beyond 1911, the youngest was Gladys Winifred Bird born in 1909. There are no Gladys Winifred Birds, there are 158 Gladys Birds and 28 with a George in the same household. The next child was Stanley George Bird (born 1897, died 1918) which generates 9 hits (either George Stanley or Stanley George) but none of the right age. In fact with none of the family were the second or third forenames used.

The next child was my grandmother Zilpah Mary Ann Bird (1892 – 1972) - a lovely name that can cause problems with some transcriptions as Z is so rare as a first letter. Yet there is only one Zilpah Bird (none under the full name), and she is the right one. Not a lot of use as it turns out that she was in service, which was news to my mother! Her elder sister, Elsie Maria Bird, finds only two, of which one is of the right age and is, in fact her under her full name, in service, and in the next house to her sister Zilpah. (If you are wondering where the name Zilpah comes from it is in the book of Genesis).

In all of the above examples I simply used the name with no other information and looked down the list of ages afterwards. It doesn't take long to skim down a list and is even quicker if you sort it into date order. If I add in the county of birth rather than the exact place, then the numbers reduce significantly. George Bird born in Suffolk reduces it to just 65. By adding his year of birth of 1867 +/- 3 years, we are down to 7. Hopefully that will give you an idea of how to play with the search and get some good results using the minimum of information.

How common is the name?

If the name seems unusual why not try searching for just the last name or first names. You would be surprised how few entries you will find at times. In some ways the more unusual the name, the more likely it is to be mis-transcribed. If you want a comparison use one on the earlier censuses to get an idea. You can, of course, use the www.findmypast.com web site to check the earlier censuses and use your credits there as well if need be.

In the case of Zilpah mentioned above searching on that name generates only 443 entries. As it could be spelled 'Zilpha' as well, an advanced search for names starting with Zilp will generate a list of 871. If you then add in the age you will reduce the list.

One custom that I am sure we have all come across is the tradition of passing on the wife's maiden name as a first name for one or more of the children. It might not have been given to them all, but maybe to the odd one. Now whilst it won't work with all surnames it might just provide that link that you hadn't thought of.

There is one thing that I have noticed over the years in looking at Halstead, and its variants, as a first name. If it is the only first name then you obviously don't have a problem, however, if it is a second name then it will appear and disappear in different records and makes finding them even more difficult.

Whilst on the subject of names, the best way to find households is not necessarily to look for the head of the household first. Start by looking for the one with the most uncommon name and then work with the others afterwards. Try looking for two uncommon first names in the same household. For example, there are only 83 households that have a Daisy and a Jonathan living together and that is without using any other information.

Missing from the family home
In previous censuses the problem has always been the men, normally those between the ages of 16 and 26, that can't be found. A lot are likely to have been in the army and therefore possibly abroad and not included. These of course are included in the 1911 census for the first time. The problems this time are more likely to be the women!

The suffragettes, as part of their protest against the government's continued refusal to grant women the vote, organised a mass boycott of the 1911 census. The exact number not listed in the schedules will never be fully known, but it is estimated that thousands of women may be missing. Many women were not listed on the census at all, because they stayed away from the family home all night. These, of course, will now be untraceable.

In other cases, the head of the household refused to list the female household members on the form. The presence of females in the house may be indicated by a statement notifying the enumerator of their refusal to complete the census, or by a protest slogan on the form; but the personal details of the females and their numbers were not recorded.

Mis-transcription

The first point to make is that the 1911 census, like all of the others maintained by FindMyPast, is supposed to be a true transcript – that is a character by character representation of the original. Those of us who have been using all the previous census indexes for a while are well aware of transcription errors – that is where the person doing the transcribing has made an error in reading the image. They have happened all too often in every census, but it isn't just the census that suffers; it is anything that involves the transcription of large quantities of handwriting.

The previous censuses were a little easier than the 1911 in that you had fewer sets of handwriting to deal with and also, when transcribing, you had plenty of other examples on the pages to compare with a difficult letter or word. With the 1911 you may have only a single line to deal with or perhaps half a dozen if you are lucky. Obviously you will find larger schedules, but these are likely to be establishments and the writing is hopefully going to be clearer.

Because there are so many different sets of handwriting with the 1911 census you are likely to end up with just as many errors, even though you could argue that the standard of writing should have improved by 1911. With eight million different sets of handwriting, transcription of the 1911 census will throw up just as many errors as the previous ones.

So what can you look out for? There are always certain letters that can be confused and the following are the more common ones:

a & o,	n & w,	e, s, & r at the end of a name.
a & u,	w & vi,	rn and m,
n & u,	k & h,	nn & m,
y & p,		
L & S,	M & W,	R & K,

And remember that some people did not dot their 'i's or cross their 't's.

Let us assume that you are looking for Jannette Sims aged about 62 and supposedly living in Sussex. We can start by looking for her using that but she doesn't exist as such. It is always possible that she isn't in Sussex at all but let's explore Sussex first. Now Jannette isn't that common a name and searching for just a Jannette living in Sussex shows only 11 entries, the first of which are shown here.

Schedule type	Last names	First names	Sex	Birth year	Age in 1911	District / other	County / other
HOUSEHOLD	CAHILL	ANNIE JANNETTE	F	1889	22	Lewes	Sussex
HOUSEHOLD	CONSTABLE	JANNETTE	F	1899	12	Hambledon	Surrey
HOUSEHOLD	FORBES	JANNETTE	F	1868	43	Eastbourne	Sussex
HOUSEHOLD	JEFFERY	JANNETTE ELLIOTTE	F	1878	33	Eastbourne	Sussex
HOUSEHOLD	LIMS	JANNETTE	F	1849	62	Hastings	Sussex
HOUSEHOLD	MILLS	MARY JANNETTE	F	1867	44	East Preston	Sussex
HOUSEHOLD	NORTON	JANNETTE A	F	1868	43	Steyning	Sussex
HOUSEHOLD	PASS	MS JANNETTE	F	1862	49	Steyning	Sussex
HOUSEHOLD	STREETER	ADA JANNETTE	F	1869	42	Hastings	Sussex

Figure 8-1 Index entries for Jannettes living in Sussex

Looking down this list we can confirm that there certainly isn't a Jannette Sims. However, if we remember one of the common errors in transcription is capital L and S, there is a LIMS. The transcript doesn't show a great deal more but the image shows all.

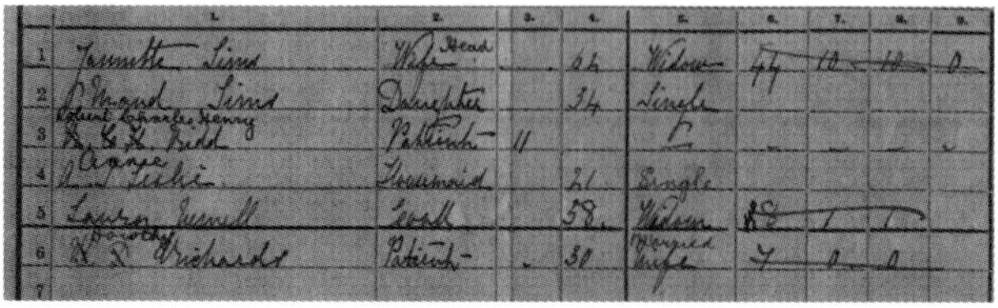

Figure 8-2 Image for Jannette Sims in St Leonards, Sussex

If you compare the S at the start of Sims with the S at the start of Single it confirms the transcription error. You will also note that the Enumerator has crossed out the details of the fertility of the three women, but at least we can still read them!

Transposition errors

There is a second type of transcription error which to be more accurate is a transposition error. This is where the person doing the transcription has read the word correctly but has mis-typed it. Let me illustrate this with some examples from the past.

Geroge for George, Willaim for William, Jospeh for Joseph, Sarha for Sarah, hopefully you will have got the idea. In all of these cases if you search for the correct name, using the variant spelling option in the advanced search, it will find the mis-spelling as it is one that they are aware off.

Now at the time of writing, there isn't a single Geroge, Jospeh, or Willaim but there are ninety five 'Laice' instead of Alice. For anyone who is a touch typist it will be obvious why the error has occurred: it is the classic hand-swap and the brain working faster than the fingers. In the first few of these examples, they are now well known and I am sure that the quality control process is picking them up. I suspect that they are changed globally on the basis that they aren't valid names in the first place. In the case of Laice it is a new one on me and definitely a transposition of Alice (I checked the first three images to make sure) and hence, I suspect the reason that it isn't being corrected.

It is of course quite possible that by the time you read this, these names will have been corrected, but to prove that they are there, here is the transcription and image for Alice Ainsworth living in Mellor in Derbyshire.

Name:	Relationship to head:	Marital Status:	Years married:	Sex:	Age in 1911:	Occupation:	Where born:
AINSWORTH, EDWARD ERNEST	HEAD	MARRIED		M	38	AGENT	LANCS MANCHESTER
AINSWORTH, LAICE	WIFE	MARRIED	14	F	37		LANCS MANCHESTER

Figure 8-3 Transcription for Alice Ainsworth as Laice

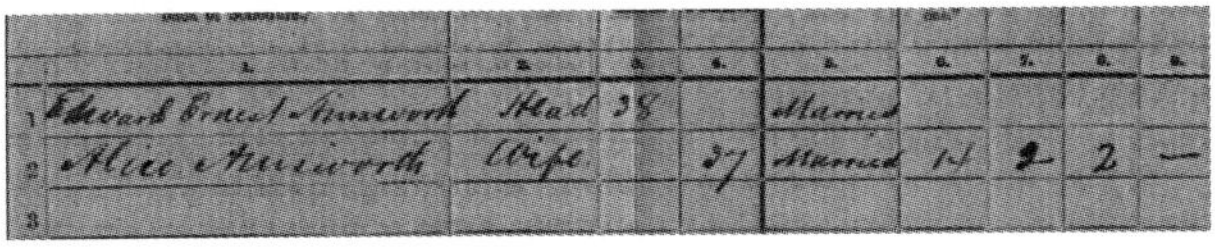

Figure 8-4 Image of the entry for Alice Ainsworth

Mis-spelt by the householder

However, not all of the entries which appear to be transposition errors are. Let us assume again for the minute that we are looking for John Bearers aged about 76. A search for him under that name shows that he appears to be missing. If we widen the search and look for all Bearers with a first name that starts with J there are only two entries as shown below.

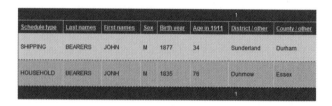

Figure 8-5 The index for John Bearers

Now the one that matches the age has a first name of Jonh not John and one could think that it is a transcription error.

Figure 8-6 Image for the household of John Bearers

The image though clearly shows that it was the head of the household who spelt it wrongly. Hopefully this goes to illustrate that just because the transcript isn't what you expect the name to be you can't assume that it is wrong without looking at the image.

Should they all be listed!

Earlier I mentioned that it had been noticed that some households included the details of dead children. When I mentioned it to Jeanne Bunting, she told me that she had two examples in her own family.

Name:	Relationship to head:	Marital Status:	Years married:	Sex:	Age in 1911:	Occupation:	Where born:
BRADFORD, HARRY JONH	HEAD	MARRIED		M	35	GENERAL LABOURER	BENFLEET ESSEX
BRADFORD, FLORENCE MARY	WIFE	MARRIED	13	F	33		WAKERING ESSEX
BRADFORD, FLORENCE MAUD	DAUGHTER	SINGLE		F	13		SOUTHEND ESSEX
BRADFORD, ADA EMILY	DAUGHTER	SINGLE		F	11		SOUTHEND ESSEX
BRADFORD, EDITH	DAUGHTER	SINGLE		F	5		SOUTHEND ESSEX
BRADFORD, DORIS LILIAN	DAUGHTER	SINGLE		F	2		SOUTHEND ESSEX
BRADFORD, ANNIE EMMA	DAUGHTER	SINGLE		F	21 DAYS		SOUTHEND ESSEX

Figure 8-7 Index for Harry John Bradford

This is the transcript of the household of her mother, Doris Lilian Bradford, with her parents. It looks like a perfectly normal family until you look at the image below.

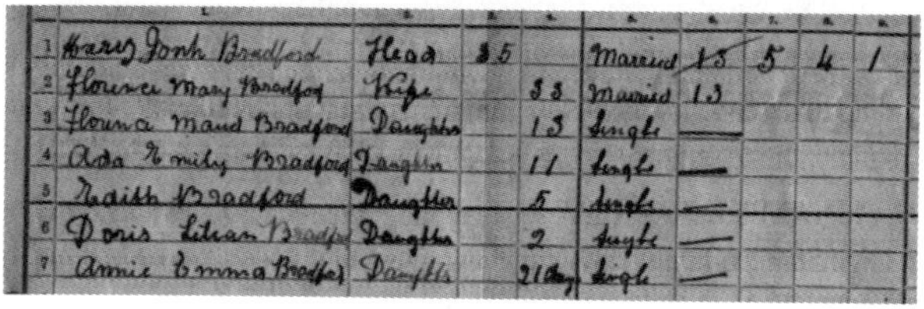

Figure 8-8 Image of the entry for Harry John Bradford

It states that the couple have been married for thirteen years, have had five children of whom only four are alive but goes on to list all five children. Jeanne was aware that there was a child who had died, but not where and when. She did however know the first four of the children listed. With a common last name it was never going to be easy to find, so perhaps her grandfather was thinking of the later generations even then.

The interest doesn't only lie with the fact that Annie had died. It says that she was 21 days old and therefore you would go looking for a birth in 1911. However, Annie was born and died in the December quarter of 1903 – the 21 days is obviously how long she had lived.

Back in January when this was first noticed there was considerable correspondence on the Guild of One-Name Studies mailing list. In the end the answer was provided by Dave Annal, who is a Guild member but also works at The National Archives and he provide the following answer which I quote with his permission.

The GRO were certainly aware of the potential for misunderstanding. A memorandum issued to Registrars after the census had been taken (and brought to my attention by my colleague Audrey Collins) includes the following statement:

"There is reason to believe that the entering of the number of children in columns 7-9 has caused some confusion to the Occupier: and that in some cases, he may have erroneously included among the Occupants of the dwelling on census night, children who were absent and even children who had died"

It goes on to say:

"If you have any reason to suspect that the mistake described has been made in a considerable number of instances the Registrar General suggests that you should test some of the Schedules in one or other of the following ways. Make sure that there are not more children entered in Column 2 than in Column 8, which would show that no dead children have been wrongly enumerated."

Audrey also uncovered a document in an RG file at Kew (RG 27/8 p.131) entitled "INSTRUCTIONS TO CLERKS EMPLOYED ON REVISION OF SCHEDULES, CODING AND INSTITUTIONS". Under Section II - Examination of Schedules part (2) Columns 6, 7, 8 and 9 there is the following direction:

"Examine the entries relating to the number of children born alive, the number living, and the number dead. If the number of children described, either as son or daughter in Column 2 and returned as being within the age covered by the period in Column 6, exceeds the number entered in Column 8 by that given in Column 9, examine the schedule for evidence indicating which children are deceased. If any direct evidence be found of an erroneous entry, the entry must be deleted, the totals at the foot of the schedule corrected, and a record kept on Form P.13 for the correction of the Summary Book. If there are more than two cases per thousand persons where such evidence is absent, the schedules for the enumeration district must be handed to the superintendent for further inquiry."

So now you know.

Nicknames & diminutives

I suspect that we are all aware that not all of our ancestors were known by the name that they were given at birth. It could be a name that they were given in the army – my grandfather was always known as Don yet was Alfred Charles Donovan, my wife's grandmother was born Alice Maud Antcliff but always seems to have used the name Lily.

There are many others including
Rob or Bob for Robert
Ed, Eddy or Ned for Edward or Edwin
Fanny for Frances
Frank for Francis
Molly or Polly for Mary
Beth, Liz, Liza, Eliza for Elizabeth
Nancy for Ann(e)
Pat or Patty for Martha
Peg or Peggy for Margaret
Harriett or Hetty for Henrietta
Nell for Eleanor
Jack for John

There is one other that my mother tells me was quite common yet I can't find it defined anywhere and that is Wag for Charles.

Can't find the street?

As I mentioned in Chapter 4, the implementation team will be looking more fully into the problems of trying to identify addresses more accurately. The problem is partly caused as I said by taking the address from the schedule rather than the Enumerators' Summary Books.

There is one method that you can use to help try and find them. You need to get hold of a trade directory for the period. You could try the historical directories website www.historicaldirectories.org or one of the many companies that sell copies on CDRom. Having found the street, you may not find your ancestor in it, but you will hopefully have the names of neighbours and can look them up on the census. With the 1911 census site this is not a cheap option but it may be the only way to find it for the present.

You will also have seen that the lists of schedules in the Enumerators' Summary Books do show the uninhabited properties so that may also help.

As I mentioned earlier there are also the streets that changed their names. For a guide to some in London you could try London Street Atlas - Historical Edition available from Geographers' A-Z Map Company Limited, 197 Fairfield Road, Borough Green, Sevenoaks, Kent, TN15 8PP and priced at £9.95. Otherwise contact the local studies library for the area in question.

Completed in a foreign language

I mentioned that many of the schedules in Wales were completed in Welsh but that isn't the only language used. I did come across this one written in German and therefore transcribed as such. I wonder how many others there are out there!

Figure 8-9 Schedule completed in German

Place or occupation code doesn't exist

I did mention in Chapter 3 that you can use the birthplace and occupation codes which are detailed on the 1911 census web site, but not all of the entries have such codes.

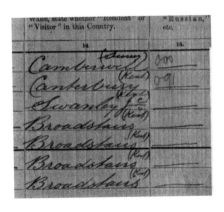

Figure 8-10 Places of birth for Ernest Banning's family

The above image shows the places of birth, several lacking the code, for the family of Ernest Banning living in Beckenham, Kent.

Relationships

I mentioned back in Chapter 3 that relationships can be a problem and want to expand on that a little here to try and sort out why, if you specify a relationship, you may not find the person you are looking for.

We have already seen that even within the family, relationships could cause problems with Francis Apperly's brother being described as a Boarder and his sister as a Visitor in the household. I am sure as well that there are many out there who, like me, were brought up in the era when friends of the family were referred to as 'Aunt Joyce' and 'Uncle Jim'. They weren't aunts or uncles in the true meaning of the word.

You then come to the problem of the wife of a deep-sea fisherman away from home for months at a time who is more likely to appear on the census as 'Head' than as 'Wife'. Similarly a woman recently widowed, if you aren't aware of the death of the husband, maybe down as 'Head' or she may have gone back to her parents and be listed as a 'Daughter' again.

Add to this the problems generated by '-in-law' and 'step-' both of which had a different meaning in those days. Additionally we have probably all come across the families where the father has remarried and the children who should really be described as 'step-son' and 'step-daughter', as they were the children of his second wife and not his, and are listed simply as 'son' and 'daughter'. In these cases they often have the last name of the new father rather then the wife's former name (either her former husband's last name or her maiden name if they were illegitimate).

We are all aware of the common relationships but where do these fit in: Barman, Barmaid, Casual, Emigrant, Man, Male, Nice or Yes? And what is the difference between a kitchenmaid and a kitchen maid – bearing in mind that you can't use a wildcard?

Finally, and with the benefit of seeing the list of relationships so far found, there is this group living in Bagshot, Surrey:

Name:	Relationship to head:	Marital Status:	Years married:	Sex:	Age in 1911:	Occupation:	Where born:
COX, JAMES	FOUND IN A SHED HALL TRONE FAR	SINGLE		M	45	AGRICULTURE LABOURER	BERKSHIRE LUNFIELD
COX, THOMAS	FOUND IN A SHED HALL TRONE FAR	SINGLE		M	49	AGRICULTURE LABOURER	BERKSHIRE LUNFIELD
BROWN, FREDERICK	FOUND IN A SHED HALL TRONE FAR	SINGLE		M	50	AGRICULTURE LABOURER	SURREY BAGSHOT
HARDING, JESSIE	FOUND IN A SHED HALL TRONE FAR	SINGLE		M	45	AGRICULTURE LABOURER	SURREY GUILFORD
PARSONS, ARCHIBALD	FOUND IN A SHED HALL TRONE FAR	SINGLE		M	31	AGRICULTURE LABOURER	SOMERSET WENCANTON
PROUT, GEORGE	WINDMILL FARM BAGSHOT IN A SHE	SINGLE		M	50		HAMPSHIRE KINGSCLERE
HARDING, WILLIAM CHARLES	IN A SHADE COTTAGE MIDE BAGSHO	SINGLE		M	37	NURSERY LABOURER	SURREY BAGSHOT
HAMMOND, WILLIAM	IN A SHADE COTTAGE MIDE BAGSHO	SINGLE		M	60	GARDEN LABOURER	SURREY BAGSHOT

Figure 8-11 An interesting household transcription from Bagshot

The image of course shows that some of these are transcription errors all of which
have been reported.

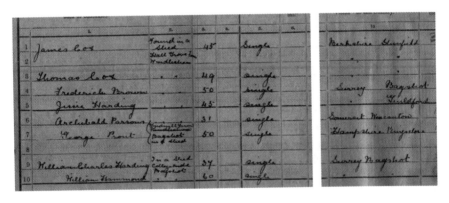

Figure 8-12 Part of the image of the Bagshot household

And finally…

None of the modern census transcriptions would be the same without its usual set
of unusual and amusing entries and the 1911 is no different.

It was interesting to keep an eye on the listings that FindMyPast issued on the 1911
web site during the scanning progress. These generated some fascinating snippets.
The problem is that, without further information, some are difficult to find but
there was:

A disparaging comment made by the head of a household about a woman in his service. Scrawled on the bottom of the census return is: "This woman calls herself "about forty" and refuses to say more. She looks 60. She leaves my service tomorrow.""

I talked earlier of the suffragettes – there is one who partially completed the form with the following

"If I am intelligent enough to fill in this paper, I am intelligent enough to put a cross on a voting paper." She also lists "6 females - addresses and names unknown" who, we can guess, were fellow suffragettes. Many attended all-night parties or stayed with friends to avoid participation.

Then there is the household return completed by the enumerator with a supplementary note explaining the sole occupant was "found dead in chair in house. Monday 3 April 11".

The return for one household lists the family cat as a domestic servant, giving the feline's nationality as "Persian". We hope the enumerator appreciated the joke.

There has always been speculation about the accuracy of some transcriptions and I well remember the long discussion on one mailing list back in 2002 about the cosque maker found in the census and what it could have been, until someone made the point that it was genuine and they made Christmas crackers.

The 1911 has its own fair share.

There is the householder who listed his wife as "slave to family".

Figure 8-13 Slave to family

Ben Ayers	Head	47		Married	
A.M.M.J. Ayers	Wife		46	Married	25
Frank L E Ayers	Son	21		Single	
Florie [illegible]	Visitor		3		
Stephen [illegible]	Boarder	56		Widower	
Laurence Giuntini	Boarder	43		Single	

Aux Postman and	Photography
White Slave	
Sailors Porter	
Harness Maker	
Plaster Moulder	for Sculpture

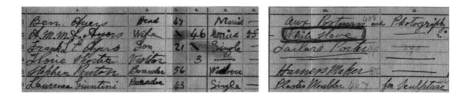

Figure 8-14 White slave

I am not sure though with this family exactly who was saying what! In the 1901 census Ben Ayers was a Photographers Canvasser and in both censuses the family were living in Chelsea.

Now there is always the odd hunter around but I am not sure how many elephants there are in Lambeth!

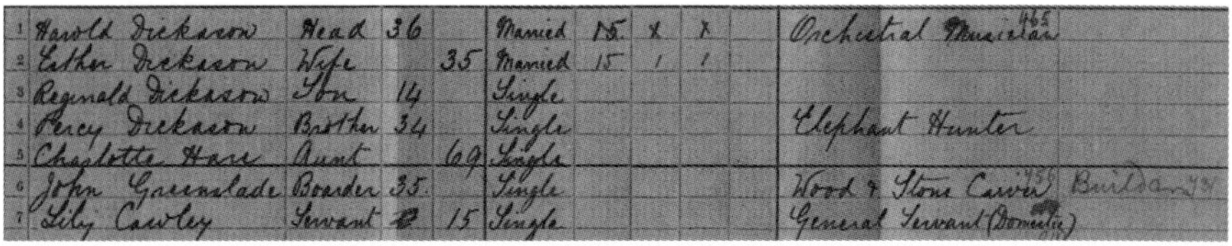

1	Harold Dickason	Head	36		Married	15	X	X	Orchestral Musician	
2	Esther Dickason	Wife		35	Married	15	1	1		
3	Reginald Dickason	Son	14		Single					
4	Percy Dickason	Brother	34		Single				Elephant Hunter	
5	Charlotte Hare	Aunt		69	Single					
6	John Greenslade	Boarder	35		Single				Wood & Stone Carver	Builders
7	Lily Cawley	Servant		15	Single				General Servant (Domestic)	

Figure 8-15 The elephant hunter

Then there is the Ascroft family in Preston where two of the daughters are listed as 'cotton lion weavers'. Now I thought that it was some new form of cuddly toy but it turns out that they are in fact 'cotton loom weavers'.

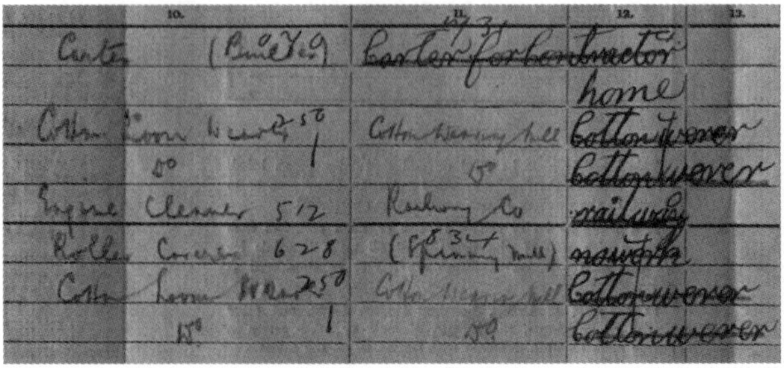

10.	11.	12.
Carter (Builders)	Carter for contractor	
		home
Cotton Loom Weaver	Cotton Weaving Mill	cotton weaver
Do	Do	cotton weaver
Engine Cleaner	Railway Co	railway
Roller Coverer	(Spinning Mill)	[illegible]
Cotton Loom Weaver	Cotton Weaving Mill	cotton weaver
Do	Do	cotton weaver

Figure 8-16 Cotton lion weavers

You will always find the odd smattering of interesting first names and wonder if they are right or wrong.

There are at present 2,561 Kings, 215 Queens (including a number of Queen Victorias and even a couple of young girls as Queen Alexandras), 450 Dukes, 1,254 Lords but only 2 Ladies, 332 Sirs, 18 Dames, 12 Duchesses, 8,049 Nelsons, 434 Wellingtons including a Wellington Boot! Not surprisingly I suppose, there are 29,777 Victorias

But I think my favourite so far is the travelling zoo that I found whilst looking for the elephants. It includes both a 'lion tamer' and 'elephant trainer', camel, bird and monkey attendants and, the one I am puzzled over, an 'animal novelty exponent!'

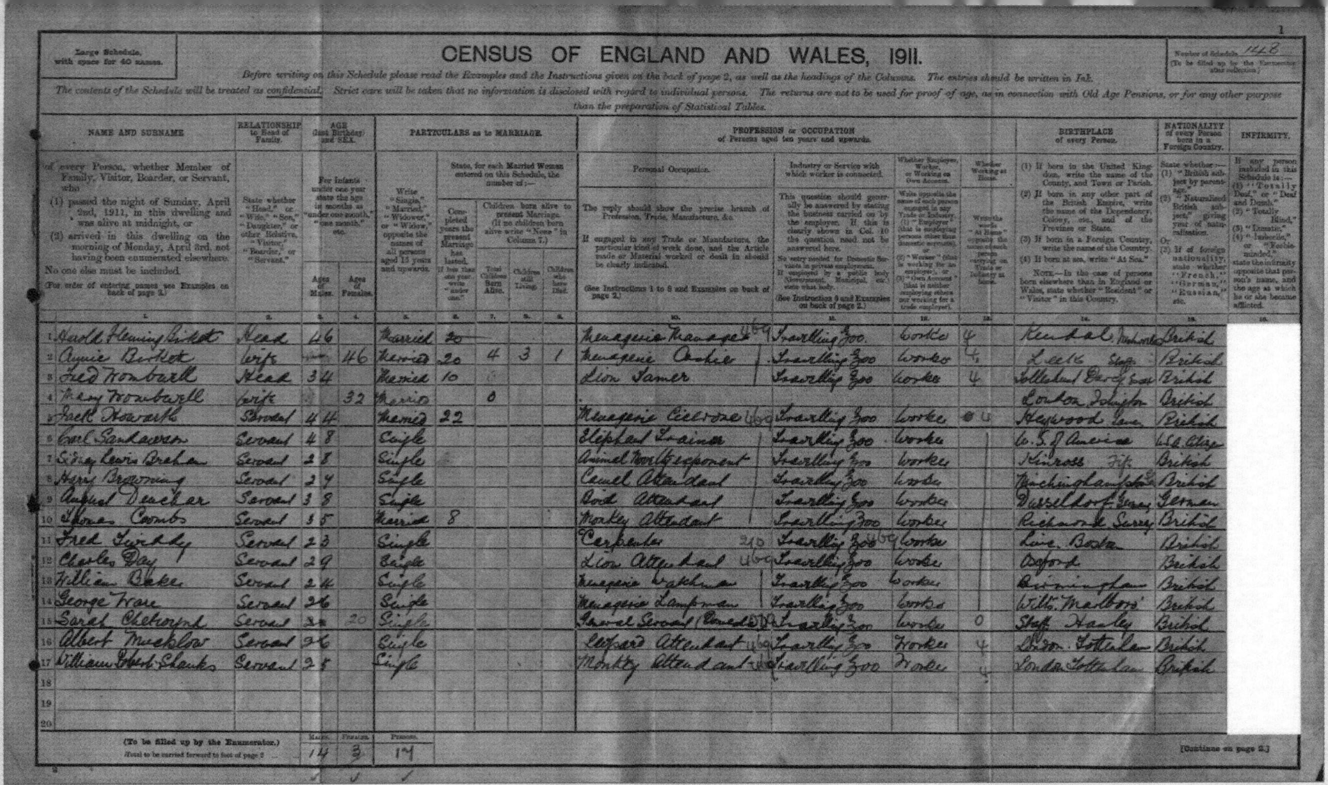

Large Schedule, with space for 40 names.

CENSUS OF ENGLAND AND WALES, 1911.

Number of Schedule 148 (To be filled up by the Enumerator after collection.)

Before writing on this Schedule please read the Examples and the Instructions given on the back of page 2, as well as the headings of the Columns. The entries should be written in Ink.

The contents of the Schedule will be treated as confidential. Strict care will be taken that no information is disclosed with regard to individual persons. The returns are not to be used for proof of age, as in connection with Old Age Pensions, or for any other purpose than the preparation of Statistical Tables.

	Name and Surname	Relationship to Head of Family	Age (Males)	Age (Females)	Particulars as to Marriage	Completed years the present Marriage has lasted	Total Children Born Alive	Children still Living	Children who have Died	Personal Occupation	Industry or Service	Employer, Worker, or Own Account	Working at Home	Birthplace	Nationality	Infirmity
1	Harold Fleming Birkett	Head	46		Married	20				Menagerie Manager	Travelling Zoo	Worker		Kendal, Westmorland	British	
2	Annie Birkett	Wife		46	Married	20	4	3	1	Menagerie Cashier	Travelling Zoo	Worker		Leek, Staffs	British	
3	Fred Wombwell	Head	34		Married	10				Lion Tamer	Travelling Zoo	Worker		Sunderland, Durham	British	
4	Mary Wombwell	Wife		32	Married		0							London, Islington	British	
5	Jack Howarth	Servant	44		Married	22				Menagerie Cicerone	Travelling Zoo	Worker		Heywood, Lancs	British	
6	Carl Sandersen	Servant	48		Single					Elephant Trainer	Travelling Zoo	Worker		U.S. of America	U.S. Citizen	
7	Sidney Lewis Graham	Servant	28		Single					Animal Work Exponent	Travelling Zoo	Worker		Kinross, Fife	British	
8	Harry Browning	Servant	24		Single					Camel Attendant	Travelling Zoo	Worker		Buckinghamshire	British	
9	August Deacher	Servant	38		Single					Bird Attendant	Travelling Zoo	Worker		Dusseldorf, Germany	German	
10	Thomas Coombs	Servant	35		Married	8				Monkey Attendant	Travelling Zoo	Worker		Richmond, Surrey	British	
11	Fred Twiddy	Servant	23		Single					Carpenter	Travelling Zoo	Worker		Linc. Boston	British	
12	Charles Day	Servant	29		Single					Lion Attendant	Travelling Zoo	Worker		Oxford	British	
13	William Blake	Servant	24		Single					Menagerie Lightsman	Travelling Zoo	Worker		Birmingham	British	
14	George Ware	Servant	26		Single					Menagerie Lampman	Travelling Zoo	Worker		Wilts. Marlboro'	British	
15	Sarah Chetwynd	Servant		20	Single					General Servant (Domestic)	Travelling Zoo	Worker		Staffs. Hanley	British	
16	Albert Mucklow	Servant	26		Single					Leopard Attendant	Travelling Zoo	Worker		London, Tottenham	British	
17	William Robert Shanks	Servant	28		Single					Monkey Attendant	Travelling Zoo	Worker		London, Tottenham	British	
18																
19																
20																

(To be filled up by the Enumerator.) Total to be carried forward to foot of page 2 — Males 14, Females 3, Persons 17

[Continue on page 2.]

Figure 8-17 The travelling zoo

APPENDIX 1
Census dates and References

1841	6 June 1841	HO107
1851	30 Mar 1851	HO107
1861	7 Apr 1861	RG9
1871	2 Apr 1871	RG10
1881	3 Apr 1881	RG11
1891	5 Apr 1891	RG12
1901	31 Mar 1901	RG13
1911	2 Apr 1911	RG14 and RG78

NOTES

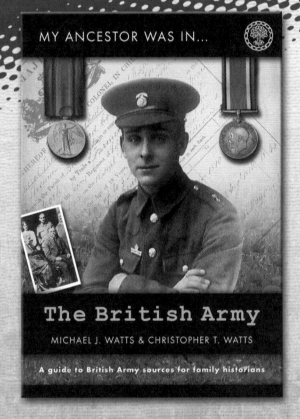